Career development:
Choice and adjustment

*Differentiation and integration
in career development*

by David V. Tiedeman,
Harvard University,
and Robert P. O'Hara,
Boston College

College Entrance Examination Board, New York, 1963

Additional copies of this publication may be ordered from the College Entrance Examination Board, Box 592, Princeton, New Jersey 08540, or Box 1025, Berkeley, California 94701. The price is $2.50 per copy.

Cover photograph by Glenn Foss

Contents

iii

Foreword

The career affords both opportunity for expression of hope and desire and limitation upon life. In America, we expect that the career is an institutionalized means for exercise of the thrust of personal advantage as modified by acceptance of responsibility for action.

Personality is also fashioned within these dual expectations of aspiration and of restraint. The career differs from personality only in the fact that we expect it to arise from more deliberate confrontation of the problem of living. The career therefore offers the advantage of choice and the experiencing of the consequences of error both of which are supposed to be self-inflicted.

The intricacies of the relationship of personality and career, although poorly charted at present, have been explored more from the concept of personality than from the concept of career. Actually the relationship is best explored while considering both concepts simultaneously. In this way one has an opportunity to avoid the delusion that the one flows from the other when in reality the two are interpenetrating.

Professor Super has been highly instrumental in leading vocational psychologists into the investigation of personality and career during the past decade. His book, *The Psychology of Careers* (1957) and monographs (Super *et al.,*1957; Super and Bachrach, 1957; Super and Overstreet, 1960), and the book of Roe, *The Psychology of Occupation* (1956), and the book of Ginzberg, Ginsburg, Axelrad, and Herma, *Occupational Choice: An Approach to a General Theory* (1951) constitute the most complete considerations of the matter of personality and career which are available at the moment.

These excellent treatises still do not fully portray the relationship of personality and career as it is forged within the process of choosing. This is the issue which occupied us for several years. However, we still try to portray only the dimensions of the issue of personality and career in this essay. Any more advanced aim is beyond our information and ken at this time.

Since career development occurs in a life, with the person participating in the evolution, the processes of differentiation and of integration must occupy a central position in a psychology of career development. This essay offers that central position to those processes. Our approach is a logical one. We have tried to frame the mechanisms which seem to be a part of the process of differentiation and of integration. We have approached with great care the matters of initiating action; and of experiencing the consequences of one's action. These concerns coupled with the concern for learning from experience also led us into careful consideration: (1) of purpose; (2) of authority; (3) of responsibility; and (4) of acceptance of the position one has evolved in life. We assume responsibility for bringing these matters into focus.

We have willingly noted the origins of ideas we could attribute to others. We probably have also unwittingly used conceptions of others. It would certainly contribute to our understanding of the matter of career development if such unions of our ideas were noted for us. Such notations might well contribute to the credibility of our propositions. We want to warn, however, that we have not gone to extraordinary lengths to trace the ancestry of our conceptions. In general we are content to let our conceptions rest upon meanings available in context or in an unabridged dictionary.

A psychology implies the power of an outside person to comprehend the probability of occurrence of consequences arising from the existence (or likely existence) of definite conditions. This essay does not penetrate the realm of this imperative very far. We have been largely content with clarification of the problem of development in the relationship of personality and career. The framing of nomothetic propositions in relation to the idiographic situation we have herein tried to clarify is something in which we trust many will share, and soon, too. The science of career development is infantile. We desire to see that science mature rapidly. This goal has sustained our participation in this project.

Our essay is in two parts. In part one we offer limited experience with career development. Our purpose is twofold. First, we are trying to draw your mind into consideration of the topic of career development through illustration. We trust that illustration will stimulate your recall of relevant experience and thus deepen your appreciation of the problem. Second, we are attempting both to establish the credibility of analysis of career development and to ease the introduction of technical terms in the second part. We therefore seek your indulgence while reading the first part. Technical terms are deliberately left undefined. We merely use them appropriately and repeatedly in order to establish their semantic context.

The second part of this essay offers more formal explication, first, of the primary mechanisms of career development, differentiation, and integration, and then, of the frame for career development. Career development is conceived as the process of fashioning a vocational identity through differentiation and integration of the personality as one confronts the problem of work in living. The closing section of the concluding part summarizes some of the research in career development. Although the research is considered in a broad way, it is not exhaustively considered. The review does offer a general summary of research completed under our direction and generally published as a part of the series entitled *Harvard Studies in Career Development*, a series in which this is number 20.

Friends have, sometimes gently, and sometimes roughly, chided us for the generality of our aim in this essay. The essay is certainly *not* a theory of career development. Neither is it an eclectic statement of available theories of career development. Nor is it solely a review of empiric investigations. Rather it is a concatenation of concepts that seem to be needed as primitive terms in a science of career development relating personality and career through the mechanisms of differentiation and integration as a chooser chooses and experiences in the evolution of his life problem. We are, of course, concerned if our present concatenation is inconsistent with theory and observation of relevance to its intent. We have not ourselves found it so but are not yet very far removed from it.

We trust that the value of our concatenation will lie in the stimulation of investigation of its implications. Implications have occurred to us again and again as we framed the essay. We did not inventory those implications and, at this moment, have neither time nor inclination to frame them. Our lack of inclination stems, not just from a sense of incapability, but also from a sense of futility.

The essential element of a career is the pursuit of intent at work. It is therefore necessary to introduce guiding purpose into the science of *career* development. Since we realize this, we now and again note that something ought to happen. Readers of preliminary drafts of this manuscript have been bothered by use of the imperative, believing that such use is not scientific. Since we are interested in career, we consider our use appropriate. The things we note as necessary ought to happen or else there will be no career and, subsequently, no science of career development. When we use the imperative we trust that it will be understood in this sense. We imply neither that all people do have careers nor that all should have careers. We merely contend that a person must think about the matter if he is to have a career.

We must confess that we do consider a career: (1) an advantage; (2) an expectation in our American democracy; and (3) even in some cases a necessity of freedom, at least of psychological freedom. We consider it unfortunate that something of such potential value is sometimes avoided because it is derisively called "middle class." It is particularly unfortunate because the supposedly upper-class interest in analysis is sought for the purpose of appreciating precisely what one's career has been. Despite these predilections of ours, however, we have attempted to hold them in check and to use the imperative as it stems largely from our interest in the study of career development as a science.

Mrs. Rhoda Baruch (a student at Harvard University) and Mr. James P. McSherry (then a student at Boston College) contributed to our work on this essay. Mrs. Baruch argued Murray's (1938) case for career and personality. There was not time to incorporate Murray's system at this moment but Mrs. Baruch's analysis of the case of Chatwell is appended as an illustration both of the synthesis of career and personality and of the potential of Murray's system in our frame.

Mr. McSherry prepared a brief of the theory of Sullivan (1953). Since we have not had time to accommodate to the imperatives of Sullivan's system, we have not appended McSherry's paper which consists of a statement of the implications of Sullivan's interpersonal theory for career development. Mimeographed copies of that statement, which is still in draft form, are available upon request to the senior author.

We are indebted to Professor Robert White for letting us share the case of Chatwell. We are also indebted to Arnold Buchheimer, Sara Carter Balogh, and the Science Research Associates for permission to excerpt and print the case of Steve as we have done.

Preparation of this essay was made possible by a generous grant from the College Entrance Examination Board. We salute the wisdom of the Board in supporting the growth of a theory of vocational development by providing complementary but not identical statements of linguistic frames at the same time. We trust that comparison of these works by others will reveal where research might profitably be directed in order to resolve differences in views.

David V. Tiedeman
Harvard University

Robert P. O'Hara
Boston College

Part I

Experience: The fact of career development

Section I. A "language" for the analysis of career development

Experience, cognition, and language

Career development refers to those aspects of the continuous unbroken flow of a person's experience that are of relevance to his fashioning of an identity "at work." The term "career development" is a linguistic representation of aspects of the experience. The primary terms of this linguistic representation are those of the person developing vocationally. The scientist must fashion an overarching language compatible with individual linguistic frames in order to develop a psychology of career development.

Language provides a medium for symbolic representation of pertinent aspects of experience. In momentarily stopping the continuous flow of experience, language permits examination of experience at least in symbolic reality if not in objective reality. The encapsulation of experience in language is akin to having only a bucketful of water to analyze and to evaluate after that bucketful of water is removed from a swift-running brook (Weitz, 1961).

Language is merely a vehicle for the portrayal of an event; the event itself is not altered by discussion of it; the event does not suffer either from its encapsulation into language or from its later release from that condition. What can suffer in the linguistic portrayal of an event is the meaning that the event had for the one who experienced it. It is extremely diffi-cult to convey this meaning from person to person.

In this monograph we are attempting to clarify the linguistic medium for the communication of the aspects of career development as they become a part of awareness. We are particularly concerned that our linguistic frame allow, in the science of career development, for both the events experienced and the meaning of those events for the person who is experiencing them.

Although the events may themselves remain unchanged when conceived or discussed, the experience may actually change. Man reacts within the context of a system of attitudes. The attitudes are frequently associated with an event and lend meaning to the experience of the event. These attitudes frequently create a set in man so that he will become aware of only a part of an event. Reflection upon an event can clarify the attitude in which the event was experienced. Such clarification does, of course, alter the *experiencing* of past events although the event itself can never be changed. Thus reflection and discussion can alter the *meaning* of an event for a person. Consideration of future conditions can also create a meaning set that a person intends to permit himself to experience in connection with events he considers it possible that he will meet. These thoughts do, of course, precondition future experience.

Finally, man can act with purpose. A great deal of man's behavior can be understood if we can but understand his purposes. Purposes are set deliberately although all of their ramifications may not be fully realized. Purposes can be modified by thoughtful evaluation of prior events. Purposes can be set anew from analyses of previous circumstances and from anticipation of new ones.

In writing a theory of career development, then, we must recognize that we strive for linguistic conceptions which will:

1. Portray the experiencing of an event as faithfully as possible;

2. Recognize that thought about the meaning of an event may clarify the experience and condition the person to react differently in the future; and

3. Acknowledge the influence of analysis and evaluation upon purpose and the subsequent influence of the purpose upon future experience.

Pattern in occupation—the career

The mind is capable of finding and of considering a multitude of ideas. The mind is also occasionally invaded by unwanted thoughts. Further, man ordinarily initiates a multitude of acts throughout his life. Some of these acts are in response to a demand from another, while other acts may be due to the will of the initiator. Where, then, in this morass of thought and action is career development to be discovered?

Thought and action can be focused. We are attending to thoughts and action when they are in focus. Attention is the joint activity of thinking and acting in relation to purpose. Therefore, attention is one of the objects of consideration in career development. But attention is not completely coterminal with career development; only some aspects of attention need be within the ken of the study of career development.

Aspects of attention relevant to the study of career development are those concerned with the making of a living and the making of a life.

Making a living

Making a living only requires the attainment of income sufficient to satisfy one's own desires and the desires of those one elects to support. Sometimes this is a collaborative matter, as in the case of a son or daughter in a family's business, and in the case of a husband and wife working for their family's keep. At other times, in addition to the customary pattern of only the husband at work, making a living assumes the form of managing money or estate for one's own ends as is the case of the "coupon clipper" and, hopefully, of the retired. Sometimes a living is made by depending solely upon the financial resources of others as in the case of the wife not in the labor force, the child, the cleric, the mentally disabled, the disabled, the infirm, and the criminal.

Obviously the expectation in the United States is that each person, in his majority, will assume full responsibility for his own welfare including his living. Just as obvious is the fact that "making a living" requires a "taking" from the resources of the world. Of course, our society tries to arrange that this taking is somewhat of a partaking of the resources of the world. Nevertheless, it should be apparent that the study of career development is a study of the ends a person chooses and the means he pursues to attain those ends as he fashions his orientation to partake of the world's resources. Career development must, therefore, involve the study of the defenses one fashions in order to sustain this "taking" aspect of his being. Such a fashioning is being effected throughout all of life. The pattern is never wholly permanent; it is continuously in flux. However, crystallization, conviction, belief, and integrity are ultimately necessary for serenity and peace of mind.

The making of a life and the evolution of existential meanings

A singular goal singularly pursued for an extended period can cause the loss of perspective, balance, and growth in life. Making a living must become a part of a larger goal if work is not to be overengrossing. "Making a life" is a relevant larger goal.

The personal meanings associated with making a life which we will consider most fully in this essay are those stemming from the psychological phenomenon of ego identity. For us, ego identity is the meaning a person evolves toward himself-in-situation as his strivings for identification with members of increasingly larger social collectivities are encouraged or discouraged and as they are expressed either verbally or empathetically. "Meaning" here also embraces values and attitudes. Therefore, the term "meanings" embraces not only the person's fundamental premises about self-in-situation but also the conviction with which those premises are held. Meanings are the outposts of existence, so to speak. "On meanings I stand. Meanings are *me! I* am my own meanings." Meanings both limit one's being and protect that being from onslaught from out there. Quite evidently, then,

these articulated premises of existence are highly relevant to a science of career development.

Ego-identity is the accumulating meaning one forges about himself as he wrestles with his meeting with society. Ego-identity is a psychosocial phenomenon. It is the crystallizing premises of existence which one forges both where one can and where one may in order to establish one's self in the world.

Career development includes the development of an orientation toward work that evolves within the psychosocial process of forming an ego-identity. This monograph attempts to frame important elements in the process of career development. A part of the frame is the biological constitution of a person. Another part is the psychological make-up of the individual. A third part is the society or subculture as it serves as a source of identification for the person. Obviously, person-in-society takes many forms. Our purpose here will be to consider only the presently more obvious points of articulation of person and society that are seemingly relevant for occupation and the search for identity.

The concept of career development is difficult to denote because it is complex. This monograph attempts such a denotation. We shall strive to make this denotation more comprehensible by asking you to share the evolving vocational situation of several persons with us before we attempt explicit provision of a conceptual frame. We shall attempt to bring to your attention relevant matters in each case by analyses which follow the cases.

In the analyses following each case we will be concerned specifically with differentiation and integration of both career choice and personality. A basic assumption is that, while differentiation and integration are proceeding in the realm that is specifically concerned with career choice, there is also a process of differentiation and integration in the realm of personality development that is related to career development. In this latter area we tend to utilize, for the sake of structure, the psychosocial crises of Erikson (1959).

Section II. Cases:
The data of career development

Structure

This section offers reports of vocationally-relevant experience in the lives of:

1. Bob, a bright boy in grade three whose career is revealed through the medium of a research interview;

2. Paul, a bright boy in grade nine whose career is also revealed through a research interview;

3. Steve, a bright young man probably in grade eleven whose career is here revealed in an initial counseling interview; and

4. Val, a bright young man in grade fifteen some of whose career elements are captured in a brief vignette of his process of deciding upon a major in college.

Chatwell, a bright man speaking of his career in his late twenties will also be mentioned in later sections. We do not include that case in this section because its analysis is not yet fully compatible with the system we are employing. We have included the case in Appendix A, however, because the consistency of analysis is sufficiently high to make it relevant to our work and because it illustrates the synthesis of personality and career so well.

The cases of Bob, Paul, Steve, and Val are each followed by an analysis noting: structure of the interview; vocational choice process; interplay of personality and career development.

Also noted are: interests; self evaluations; and interpenetration of awareness gained from experiencing life's discontinuities.

The section concludes with generalizations about structure, career development, and science.

The case of Bob (grade three, bright)

I.0: And you've seen one of these before, Bob? (Points to tape recorder)

S.0: Yes.

I.1: Tell me where you saw one before.

S.1: My father's a doctor and he used to have one in his office and he brang it home at night.

I.2: Okay, now tell me what kinds of things you're interested in, Bob.

S.2: Uh, well, wood, woodworking, umm, woodworking, painting, uh, some other things, but I can't think of them—clay modeling also.

I.3: Okay, uh, these are the things you like to do at school, huh?

S.3: Yes.

I.4: And uh, do you do woodworking at home?

S.4: Uh, oh yeah, I also like to do hemp, uh, no I do it, I do it in the fall and winter and spring at my craft teacher's, his name is Peter.

I.5: Pretty nice. Uh, there any other things that you are interested in, that you like to do?

S.5: Uuh, well, baseball . . .

I.6: Um hum.

S.6: Uh, I also like to make some things that are . . . and I also uh, I can swim. Uh, my, what I was

6

learning the other day was the backstroke and side-stroke.

*I.*7: Okay, fine. Uh, tell me, what do you think you'll be when you grow up?

*S.*7: Umm, well, maybe some kind of doctor or surgeon or pediatrician or psychiatrist.

*I.*8: Um hum. What does a surgeon do?

*S.*8: He uh operates.

*I.*9: He operates. Okay. What does a pediatrician do?

*S.*9: He's a uh child's doctor.

*I.*10: Child doctor. And a psychiatrist, what does he do?

*S.*10: He uh helps people get things off their mind.

*I.*11: Uh huh. That's good. And uh, so you, how did you come to know about these things?

*S.*11: Well, my father told me, and how I came to know what a pediatrician was, uh, every night when he goes to a party, he puts pediatricians' numbers down in case of any emergency.

*I.*12: Oh, is that so. I see. Fine. And you think you might like to be some kind of, of a doctor.

*S.*12: Yes.

*I.*13: And these are all different kinds of doctors, is that it?

*S.*13: Yes.

*I.*14: Umhum. Can you tell me, uh, what does your mother do?

*S.*14: She's a housewife and she's a helper secretary of the Republican Women's Club.

*I.*15: Does she work at that all day?

*S.*15: Well, she works pretty much at that and comes, she helps sort out cards . . . she works a lot, and she, she's a housewife.

*I.*16: Fine. Can you . . . tell me, uh, what kinds of things do other men do . . .

*S.*16: Well . . .

*I.*17: Besides your father.

*S.*17: Oh yeah, uh, I uh might be uh do something, I, I like to paint also. That might be my hobby when I grow up, or uh I might be a carpenter uh plain carpenter for people, you know, temporary.

*I.*18: Um hum. You just learning how to be a carpenter now?

*S.*18: Yes.

*I.*19: That so. You think you might like to be that when you grow up?

*S.*19: No, I think I might do it, I, I think I might do it when I grow up like um I might um do (unclear) carpenter (unclear) and paint.

I. 20: Uh huh. For a hobby. These would be your hobbies, but you'd be a doctor, huh.

*S.*20: Yes.

*I.*21: That'd be your regular job, huh.

*S.*21: Yes.

*I.*22: Fine. Okay, what sort of things uh does a uh, well, let's see, what, uh, kinds of things do you dislike? What sorts of things do you don't want to do, you don't like to do?

*S.*22: Well . . . hard question . . . uh . . .

*I.*23: Uh hum. It's a hard question, is it?

*S.*23: Yeah, let's see. Oh, I don't want to be a lawyer.

*I.*24: You don't want to be a lawyer.

*S.*24: Yes.

*I.*25: Why?

*S.*25: Cause I don't like to get up in court.

*I.*26: You don't like to get up in court, huh.

*S.*26: Yeah.

*I.*27: Okay. Anything else?

*S.*27: Uh, I, and I don't want to be uh the uh, a uh, uh, bricklayer.

*I.*28: A bricklayer, hum.

*S.*28: Yes, like kind who pick up, the kind who picks up the bricks from the side of the road, not the kind that lays bricks.

*I.*29: Um hum.

*S.*29: And cement.

*I.*30: The one that digs up the bricks from the side of the road.

*S.*30: Yeah. The clay.

*I.*31: Yeah. You don't want to be that kind of a man.

*S.*31: No.

*I.*32: Why not?

*S.*32: Well, I've heard some accidents happening. Sometimes he falls in, he gets stuck in it.

*I.*33: Um, hum.

*S.*33: And I also don't want to be a hunter in Africa.

*I.*34: You don't.

*S.*34: I might get (unclear) quickly in there.

*I.*35: Oh, yeah. Well, that'd be pretty dangerous, wouldn't it, huh?

*S.*35: Yes.

*I.*36: So you uh, do you ever talk about being a doctor or pediatrician with your father?

*S.*36: Yes, sometimes. And I also like to read a lot.

*I.*37: Do you. Is that so.

*S.*37: Yes.

*I.*38: Uh huh. Uh, what do you think you'll have to do in order to become a, a surgeon or a doctor?

*S.*38: Well, go to medical school; well, get books about it.

*I.*39: Um hum.

*S.*39: Learn all that. And ask some doctors that are a surgeon, are a surgeon already, you know.

*I.*40: Fine, fine, uh, can you remember last year and the year before, what you wanted to be?

*S.*40: Uh . . . you mean 1955?

*I.*41: Yeah, or '56 or '54. Did you ever want to be anything else?

*S.*41: Umm, uh, yeah, for a little while I wanted to be a, uh real carpenter, and a, uh, engineer.

*I.*42: Um hum.

*S.*42: You know, not the kind that goes "toot toot"; the kind that builds buildings.

I.43: I see. Fine. Not a railroad engineer . . .

*S.*43: No.

*I.*44: But sort of a construction engineer, huh.

*S.*44: Yeah.

*I.*45: You think you'd build buildings. That's fine. Not the kind that goes "toot toot". So, did you ever talk with your father about this?

*S.*45: Yeah.

*I.*46: What did he say?

*S.*46: Umm . . . can't actually remember, it was so long ago.

*I.*47: Oh, yeah. Okay. Does he like to have you be

a doctor?

S.47: Um, he doesn't know really. He says it's my choice.

I.48: It's your choice, he says it's your choice. How about your mother, what does she like you to be?

S.48: Uuh, the same as my father. She says, she just says the same.

I.49: Up to you, huh?

S.49: Yeah.

I.50: Fine. What sort of marks do you get in school, uh, Bob?

S.50: Well, we got a report card in second grade, and, tell you the truth, I got all A's.

I.51: Did you?

S.51: Yeah.

I.52: That so.

S.52: Um hm. I got the highest record on one subject . . . uh, al—, always, you know. Cause you can't get always, and I had all A's.

I.53: Fine. Okay. Do you watch TV, Bob?

S.53: Yeah.

I.54: What sort of things do you like on TV?

S.54: Well, I like fiction a lot. I mean, uh, Tomorrow, like space ships, and, uh, stories of the future like. Things that, fiction that never happened that might happen.

I.55: Um hum.

S.55: Like lightening (unclear), like the, uh, something might happen, but, didn't happen now, but might happen some other time.

I.56: Um hum. Fine.

S.56: Like scary things.

I.57: Like scary things, do you. Is that so. Fine. Are there any older people that you uh know that you'd like to be like when you grow up?

S.57: Well, maybe my father, or Uncle Peter, uh...

I.58: Or your Uncle Peter.

S.58: Yeah.

I.59: What's he do?

S.59: He's the same as daddy—works in a big office with a secretary.

I.60: Is that so. You must certainly know a lot of doctors, don't you, huh. Fine. Okay, suppose I said to you, who, who is, who are you?

S.60: Humm-m-m.

I.61: What would you answer?

S.61: I'd say a boy, Bob . . . . . ., 32 Indian Head Road, Jamaica, New York.

I.62: Uh huh, anything else?

S.62: Un-mm-m. Brown hair, um sneakers.

I.63: Okay, suppose I said what sort of boy is Bob?

S.63: Well, I don't know.

I.64: You don't know.

S.64: That film ought to run out any minute now.

I.65: You what?

S.65: That film ought to run out any minute now.

I.66: You feel like you're going to run out . . .

S.66: No! That film.

I.67: Oh no. (laughs) No, it won't run out for quite a while yet. Okay. Fine, so, uh you don't know what sort of a boy Bob is?

S.67: Hum um.

I.68: Humm um. Okay, fine. Uh, is there anything else you want to say about Bob?

S.68: Humm-m, let's see. Uhh (unclear) uh, he lives on the right side of Peters School, one closest to Bruckner Boulevard, and, uh, he has a uh Pontiac station wagon, dusty pearl, and, 1957, and, uh, his father has uh Plymouth, 1954, convertible . . .

I.69: What other things do you like to do?

S.69: Oh, I like to experiment, and . . .

I.70: Experiment with what?

S.70: Well, I don't, I don't have any experiments, but I get some things out of the ground, and, and put some coffee in and . . .

I.71: Uh huh?

S.71: . . . get some soil and some sand and put a little water in and go–, good, good coffee, and then put it in a metal jar and seal it up and put it over a fire . . .

I.72: Uh huh.

S.72: . . . and see what would happen.

I.73: See what happens, huh. What did happen?

S.73: The top blew off.

(Both laugh)

I.74: Is that so. For goodness sake. What else do you like to do?

S.74: Well, uh, read I like.

I.75: You like to read, is that it?

S.75: Yeah.

I. 76: What sort of things do you read?

S.76: Well, uumm, third-grade books. I have a book of American folklore, and a book that's called Valiant, and uh something Valiant.

I.77: Um hum. Any of those heroes that you'd like to be like?

S.77: Well, maybe William Tell, or, well there are thousands.

I.78: Thousands, huh. Okay, fine.

Structure of the interview. Bob's consideration of his vocational possibilities was prompted by reference to pertinent models: father, mother, brother or sister, other men or grown-ups, and heroes. Choice was plumbed within this social nexus in terms of interests (both positive and negative), wishes about later occupation, and reports about self. Each reply about vocational choice, interests, or self-evaluation was pursued in order to assess the limits of Bob's comprehension of the idea he had expressed and of his sense of its acceptance by those of importance to him.

Vocational choice. Bob, in the third grade at about eight and one-half years of age, is seemingly in the process of clarification with regard to his occupational choice of doctor (*I*.7-*S*.13). This alternative is presently held with elementary knowledge both of medical specialties and of needed preparation (*I*.38-*S*.39).

Bob's present preference for the life of a doctor as an adult supplanted former wishes for the life of a carpenter and of an engineer (not the "toot toot" kind) (*I*.41-*I*.45). The occupation of carpenter has been considered as alternative goals and carpentry has become defined as a hobby (*I*.16-*S*.21) and doctoring as a job in the ensuing crystallization. The definitions or organization of psychological fields in the crystallization of this particular moment do not as yet bring Bob into repudiation of his father's occupation although Bob is aware that his parents tell him that his vocational activities are for him to determine (*I*.45-*S*.49).

The line of interviewing does not illuminate the crystallization and self-definition involved in the turn from engineering as a career. There is a sequence (*I*.27-*S*.34) suggesting some concern about falling into holes and getting stuck. This concern may account for Bob's placing of engineering in a less favored position.

Although we say that Bob is in a step of clarification with regard to his choice of the occupation of doctor, we emphasize the tentative nature of the present crystallization upon which that clarification is based. Fifteen to seventeen years of schooling lie before Bob before he can experience induction into the practice of medicine. The present choice may well change in the interim. Furthermore, the present choice is not firmly grounded. Except for instruction in carpentry, life with father's occupation, and several experiences via TV, there has been no exploration. Only two, or at most three, potential goals have been examined in relation to each other in order to impose order upon diffuse possibilities. The psychological fields associated with the attainment of these several goals have not been plumbed extensively. Hence Bob presumably has a vocational goal but doesn't yet seem to have much self-investment in it.

This analysis has been organized by consideration of Bob's stated occupational objectives. These objectives, once enunciated, offer an extremely power-ful means for understanding and anticipating vocational action emanating from self-development. How do these objectives arise, however?

We have no definitive theory to offer about the origin of career goals as will become apparent as we progress. It does seem appropriate to note here that we tend to look to parents or other family members as the source of elementary vocational goals. These figures seem to be the objects of early identification. These figures are positively cathected in this way possibly because of status envy (Whiting, 1960). Such identifications lend considerable definition to a youth's vocational situation particularly when the adult, especially a parent, actively fosters identification.

Basic trust. Erikson (1959) writes of basic trust in terms of the societal meaning system. It would appear that there is another centroid to be considered in the vast swarm of meanings available, that is, the reality of self. By this is meant the personal needs, interests, aptitudes, physical characteristics, and temperament that appear to be biological and psychological premises for this person. As the person reflects on these he develops a personal set of meanings which must be integrated with the societal meaning system.

Only gradually does society impress its image on the child. The final product in the adult is a truly socialized one in the image of the particular culture or subculture. One might argue that children's judgments of many things are less influenced by social expectations. Hans Christian Andersen's story of the king's tailor is an imaginative illustration of this idea.

In the case of Bob the impact of society is beginning to be felt. Yet there is also the statement of direct naive pleasure and definition of self in a number of activities he has carried on successfully. Bob is confronting two definitions of himself—"I am what I learn" and "I am what I do." Society is making him learn in school and elsewhere. Society is also imposing its meaning structure on his meaning system. Bob's response to this is not to abandon his meaning system, but rather to distinguish between temporary and real jobs. It may be with Bob that we have penetrated to the roots of the MacArthur (1954) responsive career in which the real interest becomes an avocation while the subculture gives direction and form to the career.

In Bob's case this kind of direction is thoroughly supported by the environment of parents, relatives, and friends. It is also supported by successful fulfillment of the role of "I am what I learn." The personal meanings attached to high intellectual capacity are reinforced by the subculture of the school. In this case, happily, the personal and social meaning systems resonate together.

Autonomy. It would appear that Bob's self-control is normal for a third-grader. The incident of the exploding can seemed to be motivated by scientific curiosity rather than deviltry.

There is environmental support for endeavors in school. There is also support for exploration of roles outside of school through attendance at craft classes.

There does not seem to be any awareness of the need to distinguish between things that can be ordered and those that cannot. Attempts to lead Bob to think in terms of the future were not too successful.

Initiative. Essentially this consists of finding out what kind of a person one is. Bob's explorations have led him to define himself in terms of hobbies, sports, identification with the father's role, age, some specific dislikes and likes, achievement in school as reported on the report card, and the externals of his life in the suburb.

As we noted before under the topic of basic trust, the meaning system Bob has built around successful pursuit and enjoyment of his hobbies is now undergoing some modification. He wanted to be a real carpenter, but now he wants to be a temporary one. Carpentry still is a part of his identity at this age because he does it well and enjoys it. He is also a swimmer because he learned the backstroke the other day. This aspect of the self is quickly dropped as the context of the interview becomes clearer to Bob. *S.*7 begins an enumeration and description of medicine as a career field. It becomes apparent through a later part of the interview that Bob is growing up in the midst of a medical environment. Thus there may be an easy resolution of what may be an oedipal crisis through transference to another adult in the environment with the same role. That Bob is perhaps already moving to this kind of resolution may be inferred from *S.*59.

Negative definitions of the world of work begin in

S.23. Here again the stereotype is relatively accurate for the third grade. The distinction between bricklayers is apparently quite real but was not clearly understood by the interviewer. The reason for rejection (danger) leads to another dangerous occupation and its rejection (S.33).

Industry. In this stage self-definition is done in terms of learning. "I am what I learn." On this score there is almost perfect clarity. He gets "A's." S.36 illustrates this point, also, in a very striking way. This part of the interview dealt with things he didn't like, or didn't want to do. In the midst of the series of questions and answers the fact that "I also like to read a lot," erupted. His ability to read, and liking for it, is important to him. He returns to this point toward the close of the interview.

In S.50 he prefaces his answer with "To tell you the truth." Humility is truth and this boy had it in a very pleasing fashion. He was very bright, and knew it, and lived with it.

Interests. Bob's interests are pretty well translated into vocational terms at the present moment, as has been indicated above. His interests in sports (I.5-S.6), in fantasy (I.53-S.56), and in inquiry (I.69-S.73) are keen but not of vocational relevance at the moment. The line of inquiry about negative interests turned up the information that law, courts, and bricklaying don't stand a chance of inclusion in Bob's definition of his vocational situation. There is also the hint of fear, or at least of concern, about "falling into holes."

Self-evaluations. Bob has already learned things about himself while he is engaged at the step of induction in experiencing life's discontinuity of forced attendance at school (I.50-S.52). Bob notes that he is evaluated favorably in school. Bob has also progressed in giving definition to his own existential condition. In response to the seemingly deep question, "Who are you?" Bob first gave the usual replies, sex, name, address (I.60-S.61). As he was pushed, Bob went further. He responded in terms of physical appearance (S.62) but did manage cryptic reference to the "right" side of his school (S.68) and to some of his envy for cars. Bob did a little squirming with this question also (S.64-I.67).

This kind of question was clearly a threat. We can only speculate about the dynamics behind the reaction. He was willing to speak in terms of specific aspects of himself but the generic question was too much.

Interpenetration of awareness gained from experiencing life's discontinuities. The interview really illuminates only two of life's discontinuities, school attendance and career. We have said that Bob is in a step of induction with regard to self-development in experiencing the discontinuity of school and in a step of clarification with regard to experiencing the discontinuity of independence in subsistence. That clarification is poorly grounded and the goal distant, of course. The budding nature of Bob's present career development is further suggested by the nonexistent interpenetration of his evaluations in these two realms of his experience.

In this case the intellectual level of the boy and

the richness of the environment are synchronized. The amount of knowledge of the world of work and of self is perhaps unique for the third grade. In line after line he is saying "I am what I do" and "I am what I learn." And he translates these into career choices. He is also clearly defining himself negatively in terms of rejection of certain kinds of work. The principle career line is "I am what my father and uncle and their friends are." School and home reinforce one another, yet they do so in a manner that seems almost to guarantee the fulfillment of this boy's personality within the limits of his subculture. This is not restriction. To do otherwise might be to take the goldfish out of the bowl of water and put it on the floor so it can be free. Bob seems to have psychological living space at the moment and hence will not have his parents getting in his way as he tackles the needed integration.

The case of Paul (grade nine, bright)

Father is a lawyer; uncle designed guided missiles for the Air Force.

I.1: Well, we'd like to have you answer a few questions about educational plans and vocational plans, what you might like to do when you get older. You have any idea what you might like to do when you get older?

S.1: Probably something connected with science.

I.2: Really.

S.2: Yes. Ah, biology or go to engineering school or something like that.

I.3: Uh hum.

S.3: Or go into the Air Force and do some science work there. Or even be a doctor. That's the last resort, probably. But science is probably what I am going into. Both my uncles are scientists, my father is a lawyer, but I'm not interested in that.

I.4: You're not interested in the law, huh.

S.4: No. (laughter)

I.5: Both your uncles are scientists, huh?

S.5: Yes. Ed.D. and all that sort of stuff.

I.6: Well, for goodness sake. Where do they teach?

S.6: One of my uncles works at GE Lab. Works on the microwave. The other works as a specialist. He's some big engineer. I don't know. The one that works at GE Lab. works on cases and all that sort of thing. He and I get along pretty well together when we converse on the subject. I guess that's about it.

I.7: I see.

S.7: Oh. Yes. I forgot about another uncle. My father's, I mean my mother's sister's husband works at Raytheon.

I.8: Here in New Jersey?

S.8: No. He used to work in Chicago then he went down to Pennsylvania and then he was in the Midwest for quite a while and then he got transferred back to Pennsylvania.

I.9: Uh hum.

S.9: Probably because he got a promotion, then he went back to Pennsylvania. (laughter)

I.10: Have you done anything about this thing? Are you taking science courses?

S.10: No. I was in science right now. (laughter)

I.11: Oh! Were you? I've taken you away. (laughter) Well, okay.

*S.*11: Would this be out of line to ask what I'm up here for?

*I.*12: Just to discuss this kind of thing with you. We're interested in the development of a career for someone.

*S.*12: Oh. Do you do this with everyone?

*I.*13: No. I'm doing it to just a few people in the school and maybe in the fall I'll do a few more. What we're trying to get at is the ideas about what you would like to do and how these ideas got started. Did these ideas mainly get started from your—(cut off by student).

*S.*13: No. Not exactly. It's just that I've always liked science and I seem to get along pretty well in it.

*I.*14: Uh hum. Do you do well in school?

*S.*14: Ah—it's very funny. I had a rotten teacher this year in school. Miss Campbell. You know Mr. Porter.

*I.*15: No. I'm afraid I don't.

*S.*15: Well, he's quite famous and I wish I'd gotten him. He, ah, he's a fabulous scientist.

*I.*16: Uh hum. But you do enjoy working in science.

*S.*16: Yes.

*I.*17: How about math?

*S.*17: Oh. Yes, I enjoy that, too. That's what next year in ninth-grade mostly science and math are the subjects with the exception of English required.

*I.*18: What sort of marks did you get this year?

*S.*18: A's and B's. I get very funny averages in science but it averages out to a B this year. Last year

I got an A average.

*I.*19: Uh huh.

*S.*19: And in math last year I got a B. This year I got an assortment of A's and B's. It came out to be a B, though.

*I.*20: (laughter) You like to get good marks, huh?

*S.*20: Mmmmmmmmm.

*I.*21: Do your folks encourage you to get good marks and work hard?

*S.*21: They do! I'll never go home with a D. If I do I'll never get out of the house alive.

*I.*22: (laughter) And they would like you to go to college, would they?

*S.*22: Yeah. If we can afford it.

*I.*23: It's a pretty tough proposition. It takes a lot of money.

*S.*23: About $1,500 a year.

*I.*24: Your dad is a lawyer. Where did he go to school?

*S.*24: Columbia Law School.

*I.*25: Uh huh. College?

*S.*25: Yes.

*I.*26: I mean Columbia College, too?

*S.*26: Ah, I don't know much about that, he went to Columbia Law School and I think he went to college.

*I.*27: How about your mother?

*S.*27: She went to Columbia. That's where they met, at Columbia. And they both came from St. Louis and didn't know each other though, quite a coincidence when they got to New York. (laughter) She was going to Graduate School or something like that, and (pause)

I.28: What did she study?

S.28: She went to Graduate School, but I don't know what for. She taught art. She's an art teacher. (pause) Then she got stuck with me. (laughter)

I.29: Okay. What does your mother think of your idea of scientists?

S.29: I don't know. I honestly don't know. I suppose she thinks that's what I'm going to be.

I.30: How about your father? Have you ever talked to him about it?

S.30: No.

I.31: How about your uncle?

S.31: Well he and I don't discuss what I'm going to be, we just discuss science.

I.32: Just talk about science, huh?

S.32: Yeah, we talk about radios and that sort of stuff.

I.33: Uh hum. What business does your father work for. What company?

S.33: First National Bank.

I.34: As what?

S.34: Assistant in payroll department.

I.35: All right.

S.35: That isn't terribly high, by the way. (laughter)

I.36: Well that's all right. Sounds like a good job to me. Ah, what sort of things do you like to do, ah —(pause)

S.36: Well, I like to read. And then listen to records, you know, Broadway and classical and then, ah, I like planes a lot and I spend a lot of time with

them, taking pictures and so on. And then photography and then I fuss around with trains.

I.37: Oh, do you? Is that so? All these things are related to scientific projects.

S.37: Mmmm. Yes. I never looked at it that way.

I.38: Well they can have—(cut off)

S.38: Yeah. Well, if you get into hi-fi, well you're really getting into science.

I.39: Yes. And you have to have all kinds of engineering knowledge to construct and build trains and the same is true for airplanes, too, huh?

S.39: No. All seniors going into scientific work in airplanes go into the Air Force, take nuclearphysics and get a plane that will fly with atomic energy.

I.40: Uh hum. Did you go over to the airport there a week or two ago when they had—(cut off)

S.40: Oh. Yeah. And I blew a beautiful picture, you know, I enlarged them, of the Thunderbird, that came out pretty well and also pictures of the B-47.

I.41: Good. Do you have your own darkroom in the cellar?

S.41: I have two closets and one is a huge one so I converted that. They're pretty complete. And then I've got two pretty good cameras. I had a full-length camera for about a year and then I, around a week or two ago, got a Argus 21.

I.42: How about going into photography. Would you like that work?

S.42: Well, I don't know.

I.43: You never thought of it?

S.43: I thought of it but it's sort of ah, not too bad an idea.

I.44: You would just prefer to keep it as a hobby right now, huh?

S.44: Hum? Oh, yeah. I like to use it for my own.

I.45: How about talking this over with someone. Have you ever talked it over with anyone? With your guidance counselor or someone like that.

S.45: Oh. Do you know Mr. Murphy, well we were talking it over and they were giving this IQ test that they have and I got average marks in English and that sort of stuff and he said I did very well in science.

I.46: Well, and that kind of convinced you that you were on the right track, huh?

S.46: I wasn't thinking about it at the time so I didn't care, but it's a good idea and it's good that I did pretty well on it.

I.47: What other things do you like to do, Paul?

S.47: It's rather hard to say, ahaaaa, well you know. I do all the things—I'm running out of things, (pause) well, I read all the time.

I.48: Tell me what you read.

S.48: I read a lot of aviation stories. I've got *Tales of the South Pacific.* I haven't read it yet. I've heard the record many times. I have it, but I just borrowed it today and I read some scientific books and a lot of airplane books and adventure books.

I.49: What kind of adventure books?

S.49: Oh! I read *Time* magazine and other magazines like that and then (cut off)

I.50: *Life?*

S.50: *Life* is good but we don't get it so I don't get to look at it often, but when I see one I usually look at it. *Time* has very good scientific articles.

I.51: Uh mmm.

S.51: And then the *New Yorker.* I like the cartoons.

I.52: Is there anything you dislike doing?

S.52: Also I read *The New York Times,* that has good articles on science. They had a whole article on rockets a week or two ago.

I.53: I saw that, yeah.

S.53: That was a wonderful article.

I.54: Okay. So what are the sort of things you dislike doing?

S.54: Oh. That is, well, mowing the lawns and that sort of thing. (laughter)

I.55: (laughter)

S.55: However, I get money out of the lawns I do for the neighbors, I got five bucks last Sunday and I spent it all. (laughter) I spent it on film and I paid back my mother. Something I owed her. I have a cash balance of 30 cents now. (laughter)

I.56: (laughter) Do you keep a budget?

S.56: I try to keep the money, but there are certain spendings that I do do. We've got money in the bank and I try to keep it there. But, I don't know what I dislike to do. Oh! The piano, I dislike that.

I.57: So, this interest in science is pretty general, I gather.

S.57: I got a lot of general — (cut off)

I.58: Yeah, well, you have a specific interest in airplanes, is that it?

S.58: Quite a bit.

I.59: An aeronautical engineer, huh?

S.59: That may be so. I'd like to fly, but that's impossible.

*I.*60: Oh. Couldn't you?

*S.*60: Yeah, I suppose, with glasses. I suppose I could get in if I were to ditch the glasses but that's sort of hard to do.

*I.*61: Yeah, I guess you couldn't do that.

*S.*61: I could probably buy my own plane. A cool six thousand.

*I.*62: (laughter)

*S.*62: No. You can get a piper cub for five but those aren't any good. Get a nice one, a second hand DV—(unclear). As I remember after World War II, you could get to buy a plane for five bucks or so.

*I.*63: Well, okay. Are there any other things you'd like to mention about your future plans?

*S.*63: I don't know. After college, I'll just settle down and work, I hope.

Structure of the interview. The vocational possibilities of Paul were prompted in much the same way as were those of Bob. Paul was not asked to represent his existence, (that is, to answer to "Who are you?"), however. Paul largely revealed himself in terms of his interests; there is reference to vocation though.

Vocational choice. Paul is spending a summer at school (in an enrichment-type program) prior to entering grade nine next September. He, too, appears to be in the stage of clarification with regard to his vocational choice, ". . . something connected with science" (*S.*1), particularly biology, engineering, or medicine, presently a probable last resort (*S.*3). Paul's interest in engineering is pretty well supported by identification with an uncle, possibly a physicist, who discusses science with him (*S.*31).

Paul's work in school is consistent with his present preference for science (engineering). He embarks upon a step of induction this summer as he pursues a course in science (*S.*10). He will begin the pursuit of mathematics and science in September in grade nine (*S.*17). He has done well in mathematics and science in earlier grades (*I.*18-*S.*21). Paul hints at a sense of competence in science (*S.*13 and *S.*46). His vocational choice suggests the attitude, "I am what I do!" Trains, planes, and particularly photography are well developed interests (*I.*36-*S.*41). Paul was first struck by, but then appeared doubtful of the interviewer's suggestion (*I.*37) that these interests supported his choice of science as they seem to do.

Paul indicates some awareness of the pattern of discontinuities that stand before him, college (*I.*22-*S.*23) and then work (*S.*63). He indicates awareness of what college will cost (*S.*23) but has some trouble distinguishing between college and graduate school (*S.*26-*S.*27). Work is still relatively undifferentiated except for some definition of his father's position (*S.*35) and some negative feeling toward lawn mowing which had been a means of earning money (*S.*54-*S.*55).

Paul's choice of a career in science (engineer, aeronautical), has been said to be in a condition of clarification as was Bob's choice of doctor. Again we must emphasize the tentative nature of the clarification in both instances. Although Paul is on the threshold of induction with regard to study for realization of his choice, about eight years remain before he might enter scientific work. We expect a rather significant growth toward vocational maturity in that time.

The interview provides little or no indication that Paul has explored very much. He was surprised by the suggestion that his choice of career and his hobbies were related. There is no indication that goals have been placed in relation one to another in order that the resulting psychological fields could be ordered in some way. In fact, there is the suggestion that Paul has repudiated his father and his career (*S.3-S.35*) and has turned to the work of a favored uncle. Paul hasn't learned much about himself in the process. Yet his life situation is pretty well defined for him (*S.21-S.22*). Definition, however, is coming from the parents. Paul's pursuit of science may be accompanied by guilt unless he is later able to come to grips with the mechanism giving rise to that choice.

The meaning system. This case may appear to be proceeding on the surface, yet, still waters run deep. As this young man embarks upon the period of adolescence, he seems to have achieved a degree of integration that most adolescents will not have for two or three years more. Erikson's definition of ego identity is "the accrued confidence that one's ability to maintain inner sameness and continuity (one's ego in the psychological sense) is matched by the sameness and continuity of one's meaning for others" (Erikson, 1959, p. 89). It would appear that the two continuities in the case of Paul are neatly matched and the result is an absence of conflict up to the present time.

Paul's world is middle or upper-middle class. He lives in this kind of a community. Both his mother and father are college graduates and both went to graduate school. His mother was involved for a short time in a career as an art teacher, a career in which she could find fulfillment by giving herself so that another might become himself. His uncles on both sides of the family are scientists. That he will go to college is a conflict-free consideration except for the reality of money. Yet it is presumed that somehow this will be taken care of.

This subcultural way of life gives structure to Paul's life. There are in this way of life immediate, proximate, and ultimate goals which Paul is aware of, each to the degree of its remoteness from his present life. Meaning in life is presently derived from the enjoyment of scientific hobbies. But further meaning is provided by the existence of agreed upon goals. The interviewer gives some quick insight into the relation between the hobbies, the grades, and the career area.

Autonomy. There would appear to be a relatively high degree of autonomous effort in this case. It appears also that there is environmental support for the kind of autonomous effort that Paul makes. He says he converted the closet (*S.41*). He earns money mowing lawns and is allowed to spend it on photographic material, but there is also a debt to be paid, and here the environment encourages self-control. He is encouraged in his interests by his uncles. There does not appear to be any positive career pressure at home. At least within the subcultural limits, Paul is free, and is given support.

Initiative and industry. In some of his reading Paul recognizes the element of adventure, but his romantic streak does not lead him to consider seriously a career as an Air Force pilot. He is aware of one of the things that cannot be ordered by him, his eyesight (*S.*60). But his career can be ordered in other ways and he is considering many possibilities within the general area of science. The recognition of the economic obligation involved in a college education seems to be relatively high for the ninth grade. This may be a beneficial result of the savings bank habit. Again in this latter instance, the environment is supporting and encouraging in ways that may initially have little or no meaning but may gradually attain meaning.

Throughout the interview Paul's attempt to conceptualize himself repeatedly implies he does things and enjoys doing them both at home and at school. He was unaware of the unity of his action until the statement in *I.*37. This unawareness is perhaps characteristic of early adolescence, but the actual unity is perhaps not quite so common. Paul is doing and learning. He is aware of his success and enjoyment in each sphere, school and home. He is saying that he is what he learns. His grades reward his effort. His scores as told to him by the guidance counselor confirm his achievement record. And he is amusingly aware that his parents think well of him for this kind of effort.

Identity formation. It would appear that the suc-

cessful resolution of all the preceding crises has resulted in Paul entering upon the adolescent period with the roots of his identity already formed and functioning. Although Erikson speaks of the need to settle on a vocational identity, it may be that for American middle-class boys the delimitation of an area of interest, within which the ultimate vocational identity will be formed, will be enough. This would seem to be particularly true for those boys who go on to college since this involves deferment of vocational experience. Support for the lack of a firm vocational identity appears to come from the environment in which everyone else is doing much the same thing, and adults don't realistically expect any further vocational specification.

If this approach be true, then we would not expect his adolescent period to be fraught with tensions, unless some new value not affirmed in the meaning system of the subculture is adopted by Paul. At present such a contingency is not visible on the horizon.

Finally, it may be well to note that Paul's kind of identity formation appears to fit the modal career development pattern of the scientist that has more recently appeared in the research literature (for example, Super and Bachrach, 1957).

Interests. Paul's interests are wide (*S.*36-*S.*53) and at least those of photography, music, and reading are well developed. Paul doesn't give much definition to his situation through the expression of negative interests, however. Perhaps, Paul is making a career of agreeing once he has taken a negative stand against his father.

Self-evaluations. These have been considered fully in the previous sections.

Interpenetration of awareness gained from experiencing life's discontinuities. This interview illuminates three of life's discontinuities, school, college, and vocation. Paul is still only on the step of induction in experiencing the discontinuity of school attendance. He is on the step of clarification in relation to college attendance and his attendance seems assured both because of his school experience and his parent's pressure. Which college it shall be is not even being explored and is only a part of the clarification of the vocational choice. Paul knows that college must be compatible with the vocational objective, that's all. Paul's career development is more mature than Bob's. Paul's career development has the slight suggestion of potential brittleness, however. "They" are defining the situation except for the permitted rebellion against father (see Congdon, 1960).

Excerpts from the initial interview with Steve (Buchheimer and Balogh, 1961)

*C.*1: So, tell me a little bit—why you are here?

*S.*1: Well, eh—I plan to go to college and eh—I don't know what to take up. I was thinking of, eh—I was thinking of becoming a physical education teacher, but—eh—I wasn't sure about this—and, eh—our school, Science High, is mainly sciences and mathematics and I'm not interested in any of the sciences — perhaps a little bit about mathematics. Biology, physics, chemistry—I'm not very interested in—and eh—I want to find out what I'm suited for.

*C.*2: You feel that you do like physical ed?

*S.*2: Well, I'm eh, I'm eh, a pretty good athlete. I know that—I'm pretty sure I am anyway—and eh—I feel that I would enjoy working with children. It seems to me that it's a nice profession.

*C.*3: Hm, hm. (long pause) You like it because you like what you are doing?

*S.*3: Well, I feel that I would be good at it, because I get along with smaller children pretty well and eh —first of all I'd rather teach in a high school, not in a grammar school, because eh—I think smaller children are nice, but I'd rather teach in high school. I don't think I'd like grammar school—because I don't know. They're not mature yet and I'd rather work with somebody older.

*C.*4: Hm, hm. (pause)

*S.*4: Eh—it seems funny (slight laugh), but ah, if I did become a physical ed teacher I'd probably coach either baseball or basketball—which I'm interested in.

*C.*5: You do like teaching—working with people?

*S.*5: I don't know—I like working with people, but I don't know whether I'd like teaching. I was interested—a friend of mine—ah—is in McCormick University now. He's ah, taking a course in physical education—and eh—I was speaking to him and he got me interested in it—and eh—then another friend of mine, he's in Science High now, he was talking to me about going to Bickford State. It's a Teacher's College—and eh—I just became interested. I'm not sure though. Ah—I, I don't know whether I want to go to

Bickford, or any Teacher's College. I'm not positive about anything, I'm just shaky on everything.

*C.*6: In other words, you'd like to find out what you can do when you graduate?

*S.*6: Yes, what I should study, can do—what I should take up in college, what I'm suited for. If it is physical education, then I would take that.

*C.*7: And how do you think you are going to find this out?

*S.*7: (Embarrassed laugh) I don't have any idea. That's one of the reasons I came here. I thought this would be a help in finding my future career.

*C.*8: Well, what else have you thought about?

*S.*8: Eh, let's see. When I first came into school I was, ah, I was ah—my father, first of all. Ever since I was a child he wanted me to go to college to receive a good education and all—and eh—at that time, or, at this time—there is a need for scientists and engineers. So they say. And, eh, I was gonna be an engineer. I was positive. You know, building hospitals and apartment houses and all that. But I eh, I eh, I wasn't in—I fell off that track. I guess it was just a thing that, you know, I had heard about and I said—"Oh, I wanna be that, but I wasn't positive about that."

*C.*9: Hm, hm.

*S.*9: And I know positively I could not be a scientist. It just never interested me. All the sciences I've taken, and I've taken biology, physics, and chemistry —eh—my school work is fair in these subjects because I'm not interested in it. And I find if I'm not interested in a subject I don't do well in it—and—um —I'm certain I wouldn't make a good physicist or a biochemist.

*C.*10: Hm, hm.

*S.*10: And I don't know anything about the commercial fields. I don't think I'd be too interested in these. I mean, if I had to make a living as an accountant, or something like that—as an executive of some sort, I'd guess I'd have to. But I don't know whether I'd be interested. It would depend on what I was doing, I guess.

*C.*11: And it's hard to know, because you really haven't done it yet.

*S.*11: That's right.

*C.*12: But you do a great deal of thinking about what you want to do.

*S.*12: Eh—yes (laugh) I do. But, I haven't come to any conclusions.

*C.*13: How does your father feel about your desire now, not to be a scientist?

*S.*13: Oh, he agrees with me. (laughs) He wants me to go to college and receive an education. He feels that I should take up whatever I'm interested in—and eh, that would be all right with him.

*C.*14: And are you interested in college?

*S.*14: Ah—I would say that it was bred into me. I never thought of not going to college. Ah—another thing—our school, Science High, 95 per cent of the kids go to college and nobody even thinks of not going, except a few who are not. That school, you shouldn't be in there if you're not going to college as far as I'm concerned.

*C.*15: And you're looking forward to it?

*S.*15: I don't know. I don't enjoy school (laugh).

And, em, I'm eh, I'm hoping college will be a change from what I know high school is because I'm not satisfied with high school. I'm hoping that college will be more interesting.

*C.*16: What is it that you dislike about high school?

*S.*16: Eh—I don't know if I dislike high school as a whole. I just dislike my school (laugh). Eh—I don't dislike, well, I do dislike my school I don't think I'm suited for Science High. Hm—I'm not that good of a student—I'm an average student. I think that if I was going to my neighborhood high school I'd be doing better because the competition isn't so stiff and I'd be taking it easy—and eh—learning. I don't think I would be—be uh—the subjects wouldn't be so intense and I'd be—you know—at ease and not nervous about this guy over here getting a 99 and this one's getting a 98—and I'm getting an 85.

*C.*17: Hm, hm.

*S.*17: It's, it's, it's pretty bad, because it's so intense in my school that it gets me nervous (voice rises). That's the reason I don't like it. I don't know —probably it's a foolish reason, but—

*C.*18: No, it's not a foolish reason, Steve. So, ah, you're in Science High but you're not too satisfied there because of the concentration on the work. And, or, you've always thought about college and your parents have always thought about it—but you're not quite certain—or—you can't see yourself in college.

*S.*18: (Laugh)—No, I didn't want to give that impression. I'd like to go to college.

*C.*19: Well. Perhaps we could talk a little more about school. Do you have anything else to add?

*S.*19: Well, I, I should say that why I'm interested in physical education. I've eh, I've eh—my main interest in school, other than studying, is sports and um —I play basketball and I swim. And eh, I don't mean to brag, but I'm fairly good at these. And I enjoy sports. I mean, more than the usual, ah, things a kid would enjoy. Eh—I don't know how to put it. I get so excited when I'm playing that I forget everything else, and it's, it's part of my life. It's a very strong feeling that I have about sports—and I feel that if I did become a physical education teacher I would be helping—um—I don't know, I have the feeling, especially in cities, that eh—not enough emphasis is put on physical ability and fitness. I might have got this theory from my coach, my basketball coach. He's a bug on this, too, but I erh, especially in my school. This is another thing I don't like about my school. The kids are very smart, but er, more likely they're not physically fit. They couldn't take care of themselves in a situation where they would have to protect themselves it's not going to do them any good. It will do them—eh—some good, but if it comes down to well —physical fitness—they're out. And I believe that with a good mind you should have a good body.

*C.*20: Do you give a great deal of time to sports?

*S.*20: Em—I er—I should say—(pause)—well, I'll give you an example. During the basketball season— er—we get out of school at 2:30. We go down and eat lunch in as short a time as possible and then we rush down to the basketball field. And usually I get home, ah—at seven, if I'm lucky, at night. So I would say

I give a great deal of time to sports, especially during the season, the basketball season.

*C.*21: What else do you do, Steve?

*S.*21: Eh—I or, I enjoy music and reading. I'm pretty interested in classical music. And eh, reading I've always enjoyed. I think I've gotten that from my father. He reads a lot and he's gotten me to read. That's one of the things I don't mind about school. They make you read. I enjoy that.

*C.*22: What sort of books do you read?

*S.*22: All sorts—except I don't read science-fiction. I don't care for it. I don't know—I've read very few —I've only read a couple in the first place that I enjoyed. I enjoy more—er—the classics. When I was younger I read Maupassant eh, and eh—who else, Fielding, and so on and so forth. And I'm reading eh—just lately I've started *War and Peace,* and I enjoy reading. I don't do it usually for school. I don't enjoy it usually if I have to read a book for school— as if you know, if I'm just reading the book for myself I enjoy it more.

*C.*23: In your school do they emphasize science books?

*S.*23: Oh—you mean science-fiction?

*C.*24: Mn.

*S.*24: No, they don't. They don't emphasize science-fiction. They try to keep us away from it, I think, but oh, these eh, the kinds who are interested in science read a lot of the science-fiction, I find. But I don't care for it. The only one I heard about that was fairly interesting I think, was *1984,* or, I, . . .

*C.*25: Orwell?

*S.*25: Orwell. You see I'm thinking about something and it'll come back to me. Oh—this book, I started it, but unfortunately I didn't have the time. It was during the Project Talent and I got sidetracked. I put the book down and I had to take it back because it, you know, it was overdue in the library.

*C.*26: When you mention music, do you play an instrument?

*S.*26: No, I wish I did, but I think I don't have the time. When I was a child my father wanted me to learn the clarinet, mainly because of my uncle. We lived with my aunt and uncle. He was a flutist—is— and he teaches that. My father wanted me to learn from him, but he, I couldn't (laughing) stick to it. I, I'd try for a half hour and then I'd go out and play football. You know, I was a small boy. I wish I had learned right now, though. I was, I was going to try to learn the banjo, but I don't have the time now. It's just another absence of time.

*C.*27: Mm. You feel that school takes up a great deal of your time—especially Science High.

*S.*27: School — and the things that come out of school, like sports. That takes a great deal of my time—too much—too much of my time. I think if I was in a different school it wouldn't take up that much of my time.

*C.*28: You feel that you'd like to have a little more —er—leisure time.

*S.*28: Leisure time. (simultaneously)

*C.*29: Are there any other, er, things that you are interested in?

S.29: (Pause)—not really eh—I, I er, I fooled around a little bit with stamps, but I don't have the time. I can't get interested in too much stuff right now. There's just twenty-four hours in the day and I have to sleep a certain amount and—

C.30: Well, you feel that, although you're not certain, you know you love athletics, you love sports.

S.30: Definitely.

C.31: And you think that that's what you might be interested in doing, but you're not sure.

S.31: That's true.

C.32: And you do don't want to make up your mind right away.

S.32: Well, I'd like to get my mind made up, because eh, I feel, eh, very insecure. I don't know what I want to do and—next year—I have to apply to some colleges—and I want to know—at least have an idea of what I'm going to do.

C.33: You must have your life planned.

S.33: To a certain extent. Probably if I do make up my mind—it might—something might happen to make me change it. But at least I'm sure that I have something going for me at that moment. I feel that not to know what you're doing, you're wasting your time. Or else if I don't, if I'm not sure what I'm going to study—oh—I could go to college—and the first year —I go through the first year and then I make up my mind, I could have spent that year studying what I want to do and then I lost that year, because I didn't know what I wanted to do. If I have that year, I'd be all the more ahead. Even if I did something, if I studied engineering for the first year and then I

changed my mind, I wouldn't lose that year, but if I did go into engineering I'd gain that year. Does that make sense?

C.34: Yes.

S.34: Eh—I feel that I don't want to lose any time.

C.35: You're in a hurry to get things—You want to make the best—

S.35: (Breaking in)—of the time that I have.

C.36: —of the time that you have—and you feel it would be a waste if it was not something directed toward a career.

S.36: Yes, I think so.

C.37: You have—sometimes people don't begin in college until the second year, you know, to start their major subject. In fact, in most cases they don't begin.

S.37: Ah! (laughing) I'd rather begin in my first year—to eh—ah—I could change my mind.

C.38: In other words, we shouldn't delay the decision.

S.38: Say I er, I er—started to study engineering and I changed my mind and I wanted to become a teacher. And at least I could change my mind, but if I took up—if I hadn't made up my mind until my second year and then I started to study engineering, I couldn't change my mind again. It would be no— you wouldn't have a second chance, or if you did it would be, er, it would be possibly a mistake.

C.39: And you don't want to make any mistakes.

S.39: No, I don't.

C.40: You keep mentioning engineering.

S.40: I'm just taking that as an example. I don't

mean—umm—I'm interested in it. I'm just using it as an example. I could use physics. It just comes to mind as an example, because, eh—I don't know why. I guess because so many people are talking about the need for engineers.

*C.*41: Steve, do you do passable work in your subjects in school?

*S.*41: Uh—I do average work—yeah—I do passable work. I wouldn't call myself an above average student —not in my school.

*C.*42: And so you also want to do something that you think you'd be good in.

*S.*42: Well, yes. If you're not good in the field you work in—I mean the competition now is great and if you're not one of the best, you lose. You're not doing as well.

*C.*43: How does your father feel about the health education—and your mother?

*S.*43: Eh—well, he, eh—I haven't really—eh—talked to him seriously about it—and he eh—I think that if I did tell him I wanted to become a health education teacher he wouldn't mind. I think he'd give me a free rein to do whatever I want.

*C.*44: How about your mother?

*S.*44: Ah—she too. Ah, you see my mother isn't a college graduate, and eh—I think she'd enjoy seeing me become a physical education teacher.

Structure of the interview. Steve speaks in the initial one of a series of about six counseling interviews. This is not a research interview as are those of Bob, Paul, and Val. The interview probes Steve's reasons for seeking help from a counseling center.

Steve's stated intention is to consult tests in order to resolve his present dilemma about specialization in college (*S.*6).

Vocational choice. Steve is experiencing uncertainty about his college plan presumably in the fall of his junior year in high school (*S.*32). Four different discontinuities of direct relevance to vocational development are under consideration in the interview; namely, high school, college, specialization in college, and vocation.

Steve attends a school for pupils interested in science (*S.*14). The school evidently selects its pupils and brought Steve into a competition in which he, in his opinion, has not fared well (*C.*14-*C.*18).

Steve entered Science High, as it is called (*S.*14), under force of an intention to become an engineer. At entry into high school his vocational choice was on a step of clarification but he was not certain about it as he now remembers it (*S.*8). The choice of engineer and science was originally a part of a certainty that he would go to college and that he might as well pursue a course where people were wanted but scarce. (*S.*8).

Steve's election of science in high school brought him into a step of induction in the first aspect of implementation of relevance to his vocational choice. As a junior he now suffers inferiority from the pressure of this school (*C.*15-*S.*19) and this inferiority has turned him against engineering and science. Mathematics is still of possible interest (*S.*1), and engineering, although now disliked (*S.*1-*S.*10), still haunts him as he seeks to recapture the certainty of course which stemmed from its choice (*C*.33-*S*.40). Engineering could still be a possibility for Steve if he were to understand the sense of inferiority it has inflicted upon him and to realize that all groups have average individuals (*S*.16-*C*.41-*S*.42).

Disillusionment and the approach of graduation cause Steve to be uncertain and to return to exploration of vocational possibilities. The counselor finds that Steve already has some depth to his plan.

The entry into a step of induction with regard to his high school choice, although not as pleasant as desired, is bearable and Steve is presumably passing. College attendance is still a part of Steve's definition of the situation (*S*.1-*S*.8-*S*.14-*S*.18) and Steve remains in a step of clarification in this regard. This premise is known to be pressed at home but Steve still expresses room for negotiation (*S*.14-*C*.43-*S*.43) with his parents. Hence the underlying crystallization is probably not too brittle.

Steve's major dilemma is "What *kind* of college is for me?" This decision is no longer being guided by vocational objective as Steve would like it to be. However, Steve is greatly attracted by physical education which offers him a sense of competence (*S*.19).

Physical education is the vocational alternative Steve will most likely favor next. He has developed an elaborate rationale for it. First, we consider the several vocational goals which Steve has presumably related in achieving once again this likely crystallization. Engineering and science have, of course, been considered already and their rejection lends definition to the situation that Steve positively cannot make a good physicist or biochemist (*S*.9). Commercial fields have evidently been discussed with someone, but accounting and managing as possible in business do not markedly strike Steve's fancy (*S*.10). Steve thinks he could and would do work of this nature if he had to (*S*.10) but he finds it hard to consider doing so without having relevant experience in them (*S*.10-*S*.11).

The rejections of science and commerce leave Steve in the grip of his fascination for physical education. This is a well-considered alternative and could easily emerge as the favored alternative if the test or perhaps the counselor tips the scales. Steve is thinking of becoming a physical education teacher (*S*.1). It is a nice profession (*S*.2). Steve loves athletics and sports (*C*.30-*S*.30) and is a good athlete (*S*.2-*S*.19). He definitely puts time in on basketball (*S*.20) and readily loses himself in athletic endeavors (*S*.19). Steve evidently experiences a real sense of competence at sports. In addition, he has a coach with whom he is identified (*S*.19) and finds in sports a means of superiority over his fellows in Science High who cannot take care of themselves. A sound body for a good mind is an attitude which might well lend definition to Steve's vocational situation for some time to come. There are elements of rationalization in the situation which, unless later modified, will prevent Steve from gaining from this now favored capacity of his.

Steve offers some interesting distinctions with regard to the teaching of physical education. He *thinks* he enjoys working with children (*S*.2), particularly the more mature ones in high school (*S*.3). He *feels* that he would be good at it and introduces the observation that he actually *gets along* (I am what I do) with young children (*S*.3). His interest, which could be manifested as a coach of baseball or basketball (*S*.4), is reported to have been sparked by investigations of a friend (*S*.5). At the moment, Steve distinguishes between working with people, which he likes, and teaching, of which he is less certain of his reaction (*C*.5-*S*.5). And so Steve remains, ". . . not positive about anything. I'm just shaky on everything." (*S*.5.) This is a phase of exploration.

Identity versus identity diffusion. It would appear that Steve began the adolescent period with almost the same tranquillity that is present in the case of Paul. By this we mean that there was to some degree a sense that one's own inner sameness and continuity is matched by society's perception of one's self. Steve wanted to go to college as his mother and father wanted. Steve and his parents thought that Steve could succeed at Science High. His ability is recognized by others and by himself. At Science High ability is no longer seen as an absolute but in a relative fashion. Steve has met his intellectual match. To succeed now, to continue to have the sense that he is among the most able in this group and have this sense verified by grades, would mean that there would have to be a change in another sense—that he is a great sportsman. The result of this conflict is a sense of identity diffusion that is quite striking in its normal manifestations.

Before going into detail in this case we would like to point out that these two cases (Paul and Steve) illustrate the developmental nature of identity formation. When Erikson says that failure to settle upon a vocational identity is the root of identity diffusion the statement must be understood in a developmental way. Paul is at present tranquil. There are no oppositions or contradictions pressing upon him. His situation is still relatively open and his budding identity functions freely. Steve has met restrictions, a lack of sameness in two areas that is crucial to the unique and rather firm identity that he has shaped to date. These areas are those of sport and scholastic achievement. Paul may experience the same diffusion as he tries to settle on one of the several choices he is now considering, but he may not. Circumstances may be such as to lead him to a conflict-free choice. We cannot say. But in the case of Steve diffusion has resulted not from the actual choice but from the preliminary steps that led to the choice and from the environmental conditions that are currently pressing on him.

For Steve there does not seem to be any basic mistrust in the life situation as a whole. It would appear that he is not questioning the meaning of life in general but only the meaning of life in these circumstances. Even these circumstances he feels he will eventually have under his control. The immediate goals of winning games and succeeding in school, the intermediate goals of choosing a career, possibly of helping people—these seem to give structure and meaning to his life, although all the problems connected with them are not solved.

Again, in this case, we call attention to the sense of autonomy that develops out of environmental support. This is a crucial aspect of this case. Steve has had strong support from both home and school in his development up to now. His sense of diffusion is all the more acute because both pillars of support are beginning to topple. His grades in school do not warrant the kind of recognition that he has received up to now from school personnel. In addition to this his parents, whose chief support has been in terms of the intermediate goal of college, are now unable to support him in the school crisis because the fulfillment of their ambition for him appears to be a certainty. They are relaxing their support. The specifics of colleges and careers are beyond them. Steve is now swimming alone and isn't quite sure where land is.

These senses of initiative and industry focus around the concept of what kind of a person I am. This concept is developed by doing and by learning. These senses are continually modified throughout life and are clearly related to the sense of ego identity. The manner in which they are established and maintained is a process of reality testing. Life itself involves us in a series of changing environments and roles which result in our finding out new things about ourselves as the years pass.

Steve came to Science High with an interest in sports and an enjoyment of school, both of these based on successful achievement in the roles they require. Reality testing at the new school has led him to re-evaluate himself, to determine in relation to a different peer group what a unique kind of a person he is. There are two chief elements here: (1) divergence from the peer group and their values, and (2) this divergence supported by success in basketball. He is not interested in science but the peer group is. He is interested in sports and physical fitness but the peer group isn't. In addition to this his own personal friends are thinking in terms that are perhaps not typical of the Science High boy—physical education and a teacher's college. Grades in school that are not up to the level of his previous estimates of himself simply confirm, from the faculty point of view, Steve's sense that his burgeoning identity is not seen by others as he sees it. He is striving for integration and fleeing from identity diffusion to an environment in which the sameness of self will match the sameness attributed to him by society. His drive probably should be supported in every way possible. The ultimate result of this restructuring, or renewed resolution, of the crises of initiative and industry will be Steve's ego identity.

Interests. Steve's interests in mathematics and athletics are considered fully above. Steve collected stamps (*S.*29) and is currently interested in classical music and in reading the classics (*S.*21-*S.*22). Steve is not a musician although he now voices regret at not following his father's wish for him to play the clarinet and to be like an uncle who is a musician (*S.*26). Steve reads the classics and avoids science fiction (*S.*23-*S.*25). This reading is *not* for school. These interests appear to be of some immediate vocational significance. Either or both augur well for Steve's performance in college.

Self-evaluations. Steve voices several evaluations of himself in the course of the interview. His vocational choice is being furthered by a sense of general competence ($S.19$-$S.20$, $C.42$-$S.42$) and his actions are to avoid a situation in science in which he is now experiencing inferiority ($S.15$-$S.18$, $S.32$, $C.41$-$S.41$). This grasp for perfection raises anxiety which spills over and sometimes evokes concern about not making mistakes ($S.38$-$S.39$).

School demands too much time from Steve ($S.26$-$S.29$). Sports and Science High must fill his life pretty fully. Yet Steve reads books of his own choice ($S.26$-$S.27$) in the image of his father, and holds no grudge toward his teachers.

The search for perfection and orderliness leave Steve concerned as his interest in science wanes. Steve must have his life planned; time must not be wasted ($C.33$-$S.38$). This is why he is at the Counseling Center.

Interpenetration of awareness gained from experiencing life's discontinuities. Steve's career development is complex even at this time. School experiences, desire for college, and the premise that college study should be utilitarian are well intermingled in Steve's mind. This is why he defines his situation as ". . . what I should study, not can do . . ." ($S.6$). He is confident of his ability to succeed in some college.

Induction in a science high school turned the definition of the vocational discontinuity from a step of clarification back to one of exploration. Interest and competence are crystallizing this definition so that the teaching of physical education is likely to be the favored alternative. The psychological field consequent upon this election is now well elaborated and has many elements of strength. There is proven capability, engrossing interest, identification, and expressed freedom from parents. It is to be hoped that the school leaves similar freedom rather than demanding its due in the name of society.

The case of Val (college junior, bright)

Val is entering his junior year in college. He entered college with his vocational choice as yet undecided. He wanted to enter the College of Arts and Sciences, but the admissions standards there prevented this. He was later admitted to the College of Business Administration.

*I.*1: Val, in your freshman year you took a course in economics which opened your eyes a great deal and made the world of economics very, very interesting to you. Uh, would you say that part of this was the teacher involved?

*S.*1: Yes, I think that was probably a great part of it. That's one of the reasons, one of the things I see in myself being a college professor is to be able to, to give someone an interest like this and to send them on their way toward a career.

*I.*2: To give someone an interest like this. Like what?

*S.*2: Well, uh, sort of a want of knowledge, somebody wanting to learn, whereas when I began, my attitude was sort of, uh, well, apathetic. I really didn't care too much about education or anything, then. When I became interested in this I sort of smartened up to an extent and began to study, doing a little outside work to try to improve my own education.

I.3: You have eliminated working in business be-cause, uh—for a number of reasons. Are there other things that you've eliminated? Have you thought of working, for instance, in the government?

S.3: Uh, I never really thought about, about it, but I don't think, I don't think that I would want to because it would be sort of the same type of thing that you'd get in a large company (vague) too much, too many restrictions and, and ah, hampering of ideas and expressions.

I.4: Would you mind, uh, uh us going back over and, uh, my asking you to go back over what hap-pened in your freshman year here? Uh, actually I'm asking you to repeat it again. Maybe in the repetition you might see some new aspects of it. You came here relatively, uh, disgusted with the academic world as found in your high school, and, uh, relatively unhap-py with having to go to the College of Business Ad-ministration rather than the College of Arts and Sciences.

S.4: Uh, huh.

I.5: Then what happened?

S.5: Well (nervous laugh), I don't know. I can't pinpoint anything. There was just sort of a, I got a, ah, well, I got into classes and began talking with different students, professors, and then I got working, uh, on the journal business and . . .

I.6: Oh, you began that in your freshman year?

S.6: Toward the end of my freshman year. Hence —(unclear)—everything sort of came together and I don't know whether it was just one day I began to appreciate it. I think it was a long process and

more and more, I found myself, uh, wanting to study and learn these different things instead of having the attitude that I had to do it in order to pass this test and do something like that. I think that's when I began to realize . . .

I.7: Did the journal have an office where you could go and chew the rag with the other editors, these chaps who were in sophomore, junior, and senior year? Would you say that, that here was where a large part of your, uh . . .

S.7: Well, I think it was, ah, listening to these fellas talk and everything and express their ideas (vague) was, well, uh, sort of an incentive to, to try and form ideas of my own and, un, un, learn about these different things. I had no interest in politics or, uh, or anything. But when, uh, we so much as started talking to these different fellows, we began, I began to get interested and wanted to learn more about these things myself.

I.8: How did it happen that you got on this staff here?

S.8: Well, in one class that I was in we wrote term papers and, uh, the professor took them down there and asked them to publish them, and then they pub-lished five or six of them I think. So then I just . . .

I.9: You mean yours was one of them?

S.9: Yes, he told me to go down there one day and talk to them about it and I went down and started working.

Structure of the interview. Val is considered here because of the seemingly rapid coalescence of forces represented in his present vocational direction. The case is intended for didactic rather than research purposes and is therefore more skimpy than ordinarily desirable. We use it here because, despite its brevity, it offers illustration of a mode of analysis we intend to formalize in succeeding sections.

Vocational choice. Val, as a college junior, hopes to be a professor in the field of business administration. He is in the step of clarification with regard to this choice. Val wants to exercise his claimed capability in sending students on their way toward a career (S.1) from this position. There is some suggestion that this interest is in gratitude for a similar act on the part of one of the professors of his freshman year (I.8-S.9). In this regard, Val still lacks a certain perceptiveness and objectivity but the line of questions of the interviewer could offer help in appreciating the reason for his choice.

The line of questions revealed a little of the crystallization upon which the choice is presently being clarified. Business, government, are presently rejected lines of realization of training in business administration (I.3). In favoring teaching over business practice and the administration of laws, Val has learned that he does not want his line of action to be restricted or hampered (I.4).

Another aspect of the interview deals with Val in the step of induction with regard to this choice of field of concentration in college. Val sought admission to a college of arts and science. He thereby would have delayed his choice of a field of concentration. When this avenue was denied in the college of his preference, Val turned to the College of Business Administration where his choice of college and of field of concentration were wedded. Upon acceptance by the CBA, he moved into a stage of induction with regard to college concentration without much clarification after a choice dictated by a longing for a college. There is little wonder that Val's induction into study was apathetic (S.2), disgusted, and unhappy (I.4).

As the College of Business Administration brought its press to bear on Val's probably very ambiguous notions of business, he had the seeming good fortune to be thrown into a course in economics which he liked (I.1), to write a good paper which was appreciated by a professor who cared (I.8-S.9), and to be accepted for work on a journal in the college (S.5). Val's studies and journalistic work brought him into contact with students, professors (S.5), and fellow editors (I.7-S.7) who widened his horizons, particularly with regard to politics (S.7).

These experiences in the college and on its journals gave Val a sense of competence and the freedom to translate the then favored capacity into the vocational choice of professor of business administration. This choice seems destined to guide Val's effort for at least a first job. Has it been elaborated sufficiently to be self-sustaining? The issue seems in doubt.

Identity. By his own description Val's senses of autonomy, initiative, industry, and identity were in a rather confused state prior to his entry into college (S.2). Entry into college, as described, appeared to be no help to differentiation and integration of his personality. However, it does seem that all four senses suddenly burst forth in a rather spectacular way producing the sort of integration that will confound the prediction formula. But in another sense the case seems to lend validity to the personality factors we are discussing and thus to a counseling and guidance program based on them. Perhaps we could engage in prediction on another scale.

The interaction in this case is relatively complex. Val came into the late adolescent period apparently without resolving the earlier psychosocial crises in the gradual way in which Bob, Paul, and Steve appear to have resolved them.

Chronologically it appears that the resolution of these psychosocial crises occurred at the same time as identification with a college professor and a discovery that learning economics was enjoyable.

At the end of the first term the professor took the first step toward environmental support for Val's career by presenting his term paper to the school journal. The effect was remarkable. Now Val became what he did and what he learned. He embarked upon a college career of writing that was independent and successful.

Recognition of his changed condition came from home in the form of a lessening of restrictions and from school in his appointment to the journal staff. Val now finds his own inner sameness and continuity matched by the perceptions of him by people who are important to him—faculty, peers, family.

Once started, the integration took place rapidly. We might hypothesize that the white heat of the journalistic furnace fused the two continuities of self and society in a manner not possible in the crystallization stages of other careers. Other people's understandings of the sameness and continuity in the person are perhaps not so quickly seen in other careers as they are when one spreads oneself in black and white on the pages of the college journal.

There is also the possibility that there is present in this case evidence for the developmental drive toward integration of which Rogers (1951) writes. At the age of 18 all the elements for integration were present but there remained identity diffusion. It is probable that several keys would fit this lock. In this case the role of key turner fell to a college professor. The door was then opened by Val.

Interests. Val's interests are pretty definitely in journalism and in teaching business subjects. The interview does not indicate whether these are only due to the college experience or not.

Self-evaluations. It is quite evident that Val has an image of himself as a professor and writer. He is enjoying a sense of competence with scholarship which had evidently not been his before college. He has yet to gain objectivity toward this realization which might have brought him relief from the former doubts of his parents. At last he is repaying their trust in him.

Interpenetration of awareness gained from experiencing life's discontinuities. Val's entry into the College of Business Administration was rapidly translated into the appearance of an appropriate vocational goal. The examination has not been deep, however. Hence, we must leave Val wondering whether his choice will lead to ultimate success or not. Whatever the outcome, however, it seems that Val has gained a confidence in two years at college which promises to be of help if his present vocational goal fails to yield the satisfactions he imputes to it.

Structure, career development, and science

Bob, Paul, and Val each reports upon his life as requested by an interviewer intent upon revealing the extent and appreciation of career development evident in each subject. Steve reveals his life through the promptings both of his expectation of an initial counseling session and of his counselor. Our analyses are focused upon career development in these two kinds of cases. The analyses suggest that the present course of vocational choice can be made evident in relation to a paradigm of the process of differentiation and integration as this paradigm is applied successively to the several discontinuities of life requiring choice and commitment in education and work. The paradigm essentially denotes the delaying mechanism of decision and of action upon decision, a mechanism necessary for rational endeavor.

It is possible to choose educational and vocational pursuits on a rational basis. Not everyone does so every time, of course; here we note only the potential. When one chooses on a rational basis he has opportunity to lay out alternatives, to assess both wishes and risks, to examine favored alternatives, and to construct a definition of himself in the situation which guides his pursuit of the elected course. The existence, validity, clarity, force, tentativeness, and openness of this definition, as its actual and imputed consequences are experienced, are of concern in the study of career development. It is for this reason that the existing career developments of the four persons were each analyzed not only in terms of the vocational choice but also in terms of psychosocial crises, interests, self-evaluations, and awareness of the depth of the complexity of the situation.

Our comments upon the reported life situations of Bob, Paul, Steve, and Val deliberately reflect our concern for the complexity, clarity, and validity of the basis and motivation for choice as well as for the balance of the commitment to action so far inherent in their career developments. We have let ideal circumstances guide our thinking and have thereby set them up as goals. Are we therefore unscientific? We think not, as long as we allow the ideas to change as directed by thoughtful examination of relevant experience with their utility.

We shall in this monograph attempt, in a small way, to outline the structure of the life situation within which the definition of the career matures. Furthermore, we shall comment upon this structure in relation to the evaluation and pursuit of intent in vocational endeavors. Life and career will be put in relation with choosing. The goal is the practice of relevant and necessary action in work situations defined by one's choice rather than by one's colleagues or destiny. ("I am as *I* am, damn it, not as *you* made me be!") These exercises give rise to a number of empiric questions which we consider worthy of investigation.

Part II

Concepts: A framework for the study of career development

Section III.
Differentiation and integration:
The mechanisms of career development

The concepts of differentiation and integration

We have noted that the locus of career development is in a presumably continuously differentiating ego-identity as it is formed from experience. Differentiation is a matter of distinguishing by a specific difference; of separating an aspect from its larger considerations; of distinguishing a part from a whole.

Specific differences emerge in various ways. We are aware that illusions in visual perception are one aspect of differentiation. The field in which a figure is embedded influences the interpretation we tend to place upon the figure. Two separate parts of the same line may appear as parts of two different lines when intersected at an acute angle at their bisection by a set of parallel lines.

Specific differences in perception can also be transitory because the set of a field may vacillate after a short period of fixation. A two-dimensional representation of the contours of a concave surface can give an impression of alternately receding and emerging from the plane of the paper. An idea can enter awareness and disappear even though its retention is favored by the person.

Although the emergence of specific differences is best demonstrated in terms of visual perception because sets are so easily induced in this realm, we are

each aware of their appearance in our thought. These are the intuitions that give rise to the understanding of an experience, for instance. They also provide the outline of an essay. They are the unexplained insights that give rise to the further development of a theory. These specific differences may result from the attainment of a new capacity as when the child acquires the power to grasp by opposing thumb and finger. They may occur in the premises about one's existence which one is forming and modifying as one experiences and learns.

The interrelationships of the premises one holds about one's existence may be specified and thus mapped. So may the feelings one experiences as these premises are tested in thought and experience. The premises and their associated feelings (attitudes) which we have previously denoted as meanings are an essential element of the cognitive map of self-in-situation a person is capable of plotting. Differentiation in that cognitive map which a person develops of self-in-situation seems to occur continuously. The impetus for differentiation originates both internally and externally. Internal stimulation may be physiological or psychological. External stimulation may be haphazard, as when a person moves through an environment not specifically organized against him. The meeting of an emergency situation on the drive to work is a stimulus of this kind. External stimulation may also be planned as intended in the school. Instruction in reading is intended to cause the individual to effect differentiations permitting written communication, for instance. The intent of education is to differentiate ideas, feelings, and things in a prescribed manner and to provide the person with a more differentiated condition of thought, feeling, and action. To the extent that it succeeds, then, education has an important influence upon the dispositional potential of each person.

Differentiation in dispositional potential also occurs when the individual sets himself to consider his life consciously as a problem. In this problem-solving condition, a person takes a decision, so to speak, which fixes or sets an elected course for him for a period of time.

One of our purposes is to illuminate the interdependence of personality and career. Personality and choice may both be differentiated during the course of a person's career considerations. Hence, differentiation of dispositional potential in a condition of problem-solving is an important aspect of career development. So is integration.

A distinction is powerful only in potential until it is used. A distinction is good when it is used in proper interrelation with other relevant distinctions. Relevant parts then articulate. Closure results when differentiated parts are integrated properly. Thus, integration is a necessary and highly useful corollary of differentiation. Distinctions are fine. They are to be put in proper context, understood, and even appreciated to become powerful.

Although differentiation and integration may be thus separated logically, they are definitely interpenetrating during the evaluation of a differentiation. Integration cannot be achieved without prior differentiation. The failure of integration generally causes further consideration of the distinction if such a distinction is relevant to adequate functioning. Further consideration of a distinction may result in further differentiation. Because of this, some psychologists prefer to consider integration as merely another means of differentiation. Our preference is for the logical separation, particularly because integration is the more powerful condition, that is, adequate integration requires adequate differentiation; differentiation does not invariably result in adequate integration.

Our purpose in this section is to specify the role of the mechanisms of differentiation and of integration in career development. Our first task has been to introduce and, in a degree, to define both conceptions. Our next task is to attempt an explicit statement of the structure of the process. An explicit structural statement is a necessary guide for later empiric investigation. We lay no further claim to its value because it is a paradigm and is not established observationally.

Differentiation and integration in attaining rational solutions to the problem of one's vocational situation

We have noted that differentiation originates in various ways. One of these ways is from the set of a person considering a problem rationally. This is the condition of differentiation which we will consider paradigmatically. Since the paradigm we will develop is presumably of the highest form of differentiation, it is likely that lesser forms of differentiation are thereby included. It seems sufficient to suggest a paradigm of the process of reaching a rational decision since such is the differentiated and later integrated condition that the practices of guidance attempt to facilitate.

The onset of rational differentiation is occasioned by the experiencing of a *problem*. The individual becomes aware that the state of his present situation is unsatisfactory or is eventually likely to become unsatisfactory. A *decision* must be taken. The problem of deciding may be profitably divided into two *aspects*, an aspect of anticipation or preoccupation, and an aspect of implementation or adjustment.

I. The aspect of anticipation or preoccupation. Anticipatory behavior may itself profitably be analyzed into subaspects or steps. Relevant steps are those of exploration, crystallization, choice, and clarification. During exploration, activities are somewhat random and likely to be overly acquisitive. As patterns begin to emerge in the form of alternatives and their consequences, we speak of crystallization. After crystallization takes place, choice becomes easy and the person begins to organize and to clarify in preparation for implementation, the second major aspect of his decision which may involve the steps of induction, reformation, and integration. More specifically, each step of the anticipatory aspect may be further analyzed as follows:

Step 1A. Exploration: Differentiation implies the introduction of a previously absent distinction between two things. We are here analyzing those distinctions introduced because a person is aware that a problem does or will exist and that a decision must be reached in order to resolve the problem in a satisfying manner. The career decision of Steve was in this state. Chatwell* made reference to this condition when he spoke of learning about farming and subsistence while abroad. Goals are a primary requisite for the logical analysis of a problem. The alternatives considered, or possible, or both, determine the preliminary limits of consideration of the problem. Remember Steve was toying with the goal of teaching physical education.

In the step of exploration, as we are delineating it, a number of different alternatives or possible goals (g_j, where $j = 1, 2, \ldots, n$) may be considered. Relevant goals are those which can possibly be attained from the opportunities associated with the problem under consideration. Those goals available to awareness in the study of a problem are affected by: (1) the individual's prior experience; (2) the degree of investment of himself in the continuation or modification of his existing state and of the situation in which the problem is to be resolved; and (3) the help he may seek or be given in attacking his problem.

Alternatives or goals may each be associated with a psychological field (f_j). Such conceived fields provide a context in which choice must emerge. Steve

---

*We shall now and again make reference to Chatwell whose career is analyzed in Appendix A. Although Chatwell further illustrates the assertions of this section, knowledge of his career is not necessary for appreciation of the concepts developed in this section.

was engaging in the process of specifying the psychological field associated with the goal of physical education in the course of his interview. Physical education must bring him into contact with children, a condition he expected to like. It would provide outlet for a presently favored capacity as he knew. It would allow him to honor his existential premise of a sound body for a sound mind.

With encouragement, a person is capable of imagining himself enacting many of the situations he is considering entering. An individual can assess to a considerable degree, if so inclined, the experience he imagines in the interactions required by the situation. In this manner the individual can develop fairly accurate specifications of the needed premises or structures-in-interaction (Hemphill, 1958) of a particular situation.

People may be considered in interaction when the responses of one do in some way influence the responses of another. When two cars approach each other, one may veer to the right and the other to the left to avoid collision. If so, we say that the drivers of those cars were in interaction. A driver may also come into interaction with an inanimate object such as a solid line on a road which he ordinarily refuses to cross. Predictable responses to such a structure-in-interaction are the result of education and of socialization. However, structures-in-interaction are not necessarily limited to those which one has learned. A structure may also be introduced into social discourse and either immediately or gradually come to have the force of making responses in interaction at least more consistent and, hopefully, more rational. Although Hemphill limits his own consideration of the value of structures-in-interaction to administration, it seems to have the wider applicability which we note here. We prefer this concept of something discrete, and possibly inanimate, whose effectiveness is subject to knowledge and acceptance of participants in our linguistic structure. It serves as a useful complement to the concept of premise (or axiom) governing the conduct of interaction in situation.

The concept of premise or of its complement, structure-in-interaction, is essentially neutral, referring only to the principles upon which an interaction is seemingly organized. A person can, to some degree, relate his feelings to these premises and structures-in-interaction.

In the step of exploration then, a person can, in imagination, conceive premises, structures-in-interaction, and the effect that the presumably needed premises may have upon him. It is these premises about self-in-situation and the person's attitude (or posture) toward each that we intend to denote by the term psychological field.

Since the premises, structures-in-interaction, and imagined effects which are of relevance are given order and meaning only in relation to the goal, goal is salient for any understanding of an associated psychological field in our symbolic representation of the process of differentiation and integration in problem solving which we have recorded in Figure 1. We symbolize the condition in the step of exploration as $g_j (f_j)$.

Figure 1: A paradigm of the processes of differentiation and integration in problem solving

Time

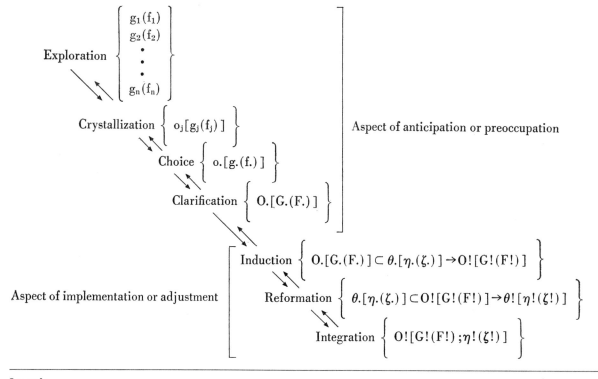

Legend:

g_j, G_j represents goal when conceived and then clarified (j = 1, 2, . . ., n)

f_j, F_j represents psychological field when conceived and then clarified (j = 1, 2, . . ., n)

η (the analogue of g) represents goal the group holds for person

ζ (the analogue of F) represents the psychological field defined by the group

o_j, O_j represents organization as conceived and then clarified

θ_j represents the analogue of O_j in the group, that is, the cumulative effect of the O_j's of the group members.

During the exploratory step fields are relatively transitory, highly imaginary (perhaps even fantastic), and not necessarily related one to the other. They may be a relatively unassociated set of possibilities and consequences.

When we apply these conceptions to career development in particular, we note that, in the step of exploration in relation to a problem of career development, a person probably reflects at least upon his aspirations, opportunity both now and in the future, interest, capability, distasteful requirements that still could be tolerated, and societal context for himself and his dependents. These are relevant aspects of the field set by each goal. In short, a person attempts to take the measure of himself in relation to each alternative as he senses it. It remains for a theory of career development further to specify the components of relevance in this step.

Step IB. Crystallization: Distinctions or differences emerge from the comparison of at least two sets or fields. Preference can be exercised and understood in relation to the competing demands of the fields imagined under two or more alternatives. The advantages and disadvantages of several circumstances can be ascertained. The cost of the several goals can be considered in relation to the return from each. The value of alternatives can then be assessed.

Steve was about to engage in this process of ordination (that is, ordering of goals and associated fields) as he brought physical education into focus in his situation. Val revealed the values or preferred existential premises upon which his decision was based. Chatwell had developed a highly complex justification of his existing crystallization.

Relevant considerations are organized or ordered in this process of valuing. This condition of the problem we denote as $o_j\ g_j\ (f_j)$. The process of valuing gives rise to values which tend to fix the organization or order of all relevant considerations in relation to each of the goals as crystallization occurs. Previously attained value sets naturally play an important part in the particular organization determining the solution a person will attain of an immediate problem. Chatwell portrayed this point well. The making of decisions intended to solve the problems of one's life ordinarily requires revaluation of former value positions and bases. Such revaluations provide a basis for the new direction probably then given to one's course in life, for example, Steve, Val, Chatwell.

Crystallization normally represents a stabilization of thought. A setting of thought is achieved which is ordinarily of some durability and hence of some reliance. This set readies the person for investment of self along a line that then becomes more noticeable. The situation becomes defined, so to speak, at least for a time. Relevant ideas from others or new thoughts of one's own may now prove unsettling and then may be accepted or derogated and dismissed.

Tyler (1961) demonstrates that this capacity for valuing exists and that its resultant persists. In this demonstration subjects first classified occupations according to the likelihood of their choosing them and then offered their bases for the classification.

A particular crystallization emerging from this process of valuing and ordering is never irreversible, of course. Sequences of tentative crystallizations, new explorations, and recrystallizations are ordinarily a regular part of the process. Steve and Chatwell both portray this reversibility.

Parenthetically, it is well to remember that each step in this paradigm is intended to represent a distinction or change in the psychological condition of the person as he resolves a problem of importance to him. The steps are discontinuous but may occur simultaneously. Hence, a person may not be highly aware of the condition of his thought at a given time. Furthermore, since any condition is merely a stipulation of intent, the force of its orientation can be dissolved at any time unless there is some reluctance about abandonment.

Because a step represents a discrete change in psychological state, the quality of the particular decision which is evolving in the process under consideration is different at one stage than at an earlier one. In a sense, a metamorphosis takes place although the force of such a metamorphosis can become neutral at any time. The former elements of a problem are present at any step but the new step changes the character of the considerations with regard to a previous step. For instance, as crystallization takes place, formerly available alternatives and associated fields leave awareness or can be dismissed from awareness.

We have represented these steps separately in our schema. The metamorphosis we are denoting is neither instantaneous nor irreversible, however, hence,

a representation of this process by double arrows. ($\rightleftarrows$). Definiteness, clarity, complexity, and rationality in the idea on which a person is electing to act can all advance or dissolve at any step in the process which is being represented. Furthermore, these developing conditions need not occur in the order represented by the contiguous steps. The progress of these conditions is ordinarily forward, however, and the advancing arrow is represented as longer for this reason. Therefore, the advance is represented as the longer or dominant arrow.

Step IC. Choice: As crystallization occurs, choice or decision follows readily. With choice, a particular goal, and its relevant field, o.[g.(f.)] say, orients the behavioral system of the person of relevance for his problem. Bob had chosen to be a doctor; Paul, a scientist; Steve, to teach physical education; and so forth. This goal may be elected with varying degrees of certainty and its motive power will vary as a result. Therefore, the pre-empting nature of this orientation in later relevant events is probably a function of the complexity and of the antagonism of alternatives involved in the ultimate crystallization. Furthermore, the degrees of clarity, complexity, and freedom generally available to the person in the solution of this problem and in the pursuit of the indicated decision will also affect the motivating power of the resulting resolution of alternatives.

Step ID. Clarification: The making of a decision ordinarily readies a person to act in accord with its tenets. Bob, Paul, and Val were all acting this way. Steve was not because he had recently dissolved a former crystallization. The person may be relatively tranquil before the consequences of his intentions must be experienced, particularly if the induction is to occur much later. This is particularly true if the conditions of the decision have previously been well clarified and if the decision itself is held with conviction. Otherwise doubt about the decision is likely to arise in even a short period of waiting (a week or more, say) for the expected situation to begin to unfold. This is particularly true when the attention of the person may be attracted to more information of relevance to his decision in the course of waiting (for example, Steve, Chatwell).

Doubt experienced in the waiting period causes the individual further to clarify his anticipated position. An elaboration and perfection of the image of the future, $O.[G.(E)]$ ensues. This occurred with Val and Chatwell. Clarification probably not only perfects the image of self in position, for example, Val and Chatwell, but also dissipates some of the former doubts concerning the decision. Otherwise it will result in a return to a more primitive step of the process. Such clarifications probably create potentials for action in circumstances of high relevance for their realization.

Obviously, the steps of crystallization, choice, and clarification, although analytically distinctive, are relatively inseparable. Disturbance anywhere in this chain of steps can quickly have its effect elsewhere in the chain, for example, Steve. For this reason, it might be advisable to denote the sequence crystallization-choice-clarification as just choice. We have re-frained from doing so because several valuable distinctions in the logical analysis may thereby be lost.

II. The aspect of implementation or adjustment. Imagination meets reality on the day of initiation or implementation; a step of social induction begins. Interaction is a necessary part of implementation. A person with a resolve of his own enters a social system which he has previously only somewhat nebulously charted. He hesitates; he looks for cues; he is inducted into the social system unless he is immediately repudiated by it. Superiors and colleagues associated with the person start the process of perfecting the projections of their expectations for him. Eventually, however, a person ascertains that he is accepted; he arrives, so to speak. A step of reformation is initiated. The primary mode of reaction is no longer responsive; it becomes assertive. As the need for assertiveness attains its desired effects, however, a step of integration ensues; the status quo is no longer challenged compulsively. Equilibrium is reestablished. The three steps of this period of implementation may be further denoted as follows:

Step IIA. Induction: Eventually experience starts; induction occurs. The individual field organized by the person's goal comes into operating interaction with society's (for example, school's or employer's) related but not identical goal and field. $O.[\eta.(\zeta.)]$. During induction, the person's primary orientation of relevance for attainment of his goal is receptive, for example, Paul entering high school; Val at the business school; Chatwell at officers school. This receptivity is practiced only so long as the person detects some acceptance of his uniqueness by the others with whom he is interacting. We might therefore expect that the step of induction is characterized by both a general defense of self and a giving up of an aspect of self to group purpose when the social system finds the person acceptable. In these circumstances, the individual's goal and field assimilatively become a part of the region (represented symbolically as $\subset$ in Figure 1) of the social system in which the person is implementing his desired solution of his problem. He learns the premises and structures-in-interaction required for continued identification. This process leads to a further perfection of individual goal and field in the social system, $O![G!(F!)]$. A ready assimilation of individual goal and field into the social purpose of relevance for the problem is probably a necessary aspect of success.

Step IIB. Reformation: When the group offers adequate acknowledgement that the new member is successful and accepted, the receptive orientation of induction may then give way to the assertive orientation of reformation, for example, Steve on Science High; Val on the paper; Chatwell in his thoughts on teaching. The person is well immersed in a relevant group during reformation. He has a strong sense of self and actively enjoins the group to do better. Furthermore, the person has little hesitancy in urging the virtues of his new-found convictions on areas of the society where enlightenment may not be as great as in the area where the person is now strongly identified. Since in the step of reformation the person acts both upon the in-group goal and field, $O.[\eta.(\zeta.)]$,

in order to bring that group into greater conformance with his modified goal and field, $O![G!(F!)]$, and upon the out-group to bring their view of his identification into greater consistency with his, the effect, if any, is the modification of group goal and field which is denoted in Figure 1 as $\theta![\eta!(\zeta!)]$.

Step IIC. Integration: Although we have characterized the step of reformation as one in which the convictions of older members of a group are modified largely under the onslaught of the intentions of the new member of the group, as exercised both within and without, these older members are not necessarily continuously passive in the process, for example, Chatwell in his law firm. The older members are likely to react against this new force for change and to cause a compromise of individual intention. If the individual is able to effect this compromise, he gains a certain objectivity toward both himself and his group. He enters a step of integration. Synthesis is, of course, the essence of integration, for example, Chatwell. A differentiation in identification has been achieved. The new-found appreciation of self is integrated with its larger field. This new part of the self-system becomes a working member of the whole self-system. In integration, individual and group both strive to keep the resulting organization of collaborative activity (represented as $O![G!(F!);\eta!(\zeta!)]$). The individual is satisfied, at least temporarily, when integration occurs. The group considers him successful also. Of course, the person is likely to have an image of himself as successful in these circumstances, too. Integration is not unalterable; it is merely a condition of dynamic equilibrium. A new member joining the social system, new strivings of existing members of that system, or a quickening of the strivings of the person himself may disturb the status quo at any time. Such disturbances, as elected by the person or as forced upon him, contribute either to his ego development or to the disintegration of his self organization.

This completes our paradigmatic representation of the process of differentiation and of integration in attaining a rational solution of a problem. In sum, we note the course of self investment in the identified periods and stages of this process. During the aspect of anticipation or preoccupation, self is relatively withdrawn from a solution of a problem as the mind attempts to set the problem in the step of exploration. Self becomes tentatively committed to solution in the steps of crystallization, choice, and clarification. In the aspect of implementation or adjustment, self is defensively invested in the solution to which committed as the person submits himself to the step of induction. Self is relatively abandoned to solution and group purpose during the step of reformation. Finally, the person again attains a certain objectivity about group purpose and self in the step of integration.

Successive differentiations and integrations

Differentiation and integration do not occur for a single problem only; this process is repeated many times in the course of a life as has been noted in all cases, even Bob, the youngest. Differentiation and integration are, in potential, a part of each of life's problems as they occur successively. Problems can occur singly, for example, Paul and science, or in combination, for example, Steve with college and vocation. The condition of one differentiation can affect the condition of another differentiation taking place simultaneously, for example, Steve. The condition of one differentiation can affect the condition of a prior integration, for example, Chatwell. The condition of a differentiation even in anticipation can affect the condition of an evolving differentiation, for example, Chatwell.

Differentiations and integrations are *interpenetrating* then. (See specific statements of this penetration in the analyses of the careers of Bob, Paul, Steve, and Val.) Because problems of rational decision can bear upon one another, we must recognize that higher order organizations of attitude towards self-in-situation can arise during the process of sequential choosing. By a higher-order organization of attitude we mean one which is specific to the ordinations inherent in the resolution of at least two of the discontinuities of relevance in career development, for example, choice of college and vocation. For instance, Steve, in stipulating that education be functional, placed a restraint upon his choice of college. College had to prepare him for something. Physical education emerged as an alternative permitting resolution of the choice of college on a functional basis. A higher-order organization of attitude toward self-in-situation need be neither of the logical kind just noted nor denotable by the subject. They may be inferred by an outside person upon analysis of a career history as Super (1954) noted in directing our attention to the importance of thematic extrapolation for a science of career development. The vocational choice of Steve is presently being directed by his belief in the principle of a sound body for a sound mind, for instance. He doesn't say this; we infer it. Also, Bob and Paul are developing as expected because the theme of trust in societal support is represented in their explanations of their career situation. It should be apparent then that these so-called higher-order organizations of self-in-situation represent the heart of the science of career development. We shall try to make this "heart" a little more specific in the next section.

Dependent decisions and career development

The described process of deciding upon a course of action, and of implementing that decision in a manner intended to perfect personal interests in the collaborative relation of interests necessary in our complex society, is possible in each decision of relevance for career development. The course of events of relevance to decision ordinarily unfolds with regard to several decisions simultaneously, however, for example, Steve and his experience at Science High in both science and athletics. Man can reflect these particular matters into systems permitting organization of diverse sets. *It is these systems of at least secondary (or perhaps of more comprehensive) order that specify career development,* for example, Chatwell. Therefore, let us speculate about the structure

within which those data may be comprehended.

How does one symbolize the thoughts of an embryo physician as a freshman in college? He is probably still in a process of integration with regard to high school curriculum, of reformation with regard to his college choice, of induction with regard to his course in college, may be clarifying his choice of a medical school (while tentatively crystallizing his thoughts with regard to an area of specialization in medicine), and also exploring issues in the election of a place in which he will practice medicine.

Career development then is self development viewed in relation with choice, entry, and progress in educational and vocational pursuits. It is an evolving conception of self-in-situation which is occurring over *time* in man who is capable of anticipation, experience, evaluation, and memory. Man is aware of some of the relevant conditions but not of others although, in the latter case, his behavior may well be quite consistent with another person's suppositions concerning such conditions.

Hence, career development not only occurs within the context of one decision; career development ordinarily occurs within the context of several decisions. Man both remembers and imagines. Therefore, crystallization in relation to selection of the first goal which led to organization O_1. can progress in some relation with tentative crystallizations concerning a second goal, g_{2j}, a third, g_{3j}, or even of later goals. In fact, the discovery of dependencies among the several decisions hinges upon anticipatory behavior emerging in relation with several goals rather than

with one alone. Similarly, traces of earlier considerations and evaluations of experience are ever present
in any later mode of thought or of action. Hence,
after-effects of all former stages with regard both to
a particular decision and earlier ones are ever present in a current stage with regard to a special decision.

The elements of the developing identity which is
expressed through work have not been specified in
this paradigm. The paradigm merely portrays the
process involved in deciding upon a course of action.
The premises held with conviction, and hence giving
definition to the vocational situation, are accumulating in the evolving organization of self-in-situation,
$O!_k$ (k=1, 2, . . . , t) where t denotes the situation
of vocational significance now being experienced in
reality. This continuously evolving organization of
self-in-situation has not been denoted in any detail
in this section. It is highly complex, of course, as
indicated in the preceding cases. The organization
of a given moment when vocational discontinuity, r,
is being experienced involves the relevant traces of
all previous organizations and of subsequent ones
under consideration. Symbolically, in potential,
$O!_r = [O!_1 \subset O!_2 \subset \ldots \subset O!_r, \subset O_{r+1} \subset \ldots \subset O_t]$.
This organization *can* consist of many different com-
binations of discontinuities.

It must be remembered that the anticipations at
a given time with regard to one or more decisions
can influence a person's mode of action with regard
to: (1) a particular decision now in question; (2)
those earlier decisions whose drama is not yet com-

pleted; and (3) those later decisions that are as yet
either being considered or are not yet fulfilled. Similarly, experience related to a present decision and
prior ones influences development of later events.
These contingencies of evaluation of experience and
of imagining of the future are probably most relevant to the matters of organizations of self as represented in the stages of crystallization and integration.

There are several theories (Ginzberg, Ginsburg,
Axelrad, and Herma, 1951; Miller and Form, 1951;
Super, 1957) about the stages through which this
organization of self-in-situation passes. Super's theory seems the best founded of those available. Even
his stages are presently not completely denoted, however. Our thought is that analysis in relation to the
paradigm offered here can improve specification of
stages in career development. Furthermore, our belief is that these stages are more numerous and more
complex than now conceived.

Our paradigm of differentiation and integration
gives rise to designation of the organization of self-
in-situation, $O!_r$. This organization offers a logical
frame for construing the feelings with which the
premises of self-in-situation are associated. This construction offers a means of assessing how a person
not only defines his career at the moment but also
appreciates the bases of this definition. This basis
and its appreciation is the career identity, of course.
In the appreciation of the bases of definition, however, we locate the degree of openness a person has
available for change of his career as desired and
needed.

As noted earlier we hold that the aim of vocational counseling is to enhance the operation of reason in this dynamic process of career development and to free the person for progress in taking and acting upon a particular decision as well as in viewing decisions in relation with those taken and those possible. In this way, the counselor hopes to bring each client for whom the counselor is responsible to view his educational and vocational decisions as a means-ends chain; that which is an end at an earlier time is to become a means for a later goal. Behavior is to become consciously purposeful; evaluation is to become more meaningful; and an elaboration of self is to ensue. No goal is to become so compelling that it either destroys judgment in situations of conflicting goals or cannot give way to a later, and more fulfilling, goal.

Differentiation and integration in the personality

When we move from the realm of choice into the broader realm of personality the degree of complexity increases by several powers. Our treatment of this material cannot at this stage of its development have the logical precision of the paradigm. The analysis of the cases in personality terms seems to us to show some of the value of this approach. In this section we shall give form to our conceptions.

Man fulfills his biological potential within the structure of his society as we have noted. Each life is unique, however, and so is the particular citizenry of the world in which one lives at any instant. Hence,

one must understand the psyche to understand vocational development. Let us turn, therefore, to one aspect of the psyche, namely that of ego identity.

The evolution of ego-identity is a process: (1) of a successively more complex differentiation of attitude toward self-in-world; and (2) of search for integration through identification and acceptance. Differentiation occurs in relation to persons, things, and ideas. Integration of personality occurs when workable propositions can be forged to link the successively differentiated elements of one's field. Acceptance and reward "fix" these emerging organizations of self-in-world.

Probably the most fundamental differentiation is made early in life. The baby discovers himself. He differentiates himself from his environment. He discovers various parts of himself that are his. He can make the parts work so that he gets what he needs.

As presented in Erikson (1959) the crises the healthy person experiences have roots in the biological order. The earlier ones are related to the classical Freudian stages, oral, anal, and genital. The crises are not resolved either immediately or once. There is an ongoing balancing and counterbalancing of forces throughout life. It is possible to slip into ill health at a later period through an inability to maintain the original balance of forces. But there is a further problem here, that of perceiving both earlier and later stages in the development of these senses if indeed they can be thought of as developmental. In our presentation we have concentrated on their implementation in later life through experience in school and in the world of work. It would seem to us that in the adolescent and adult form there is less and less of a biological mode and more and more of an integrated, or imbalanced, conjunction of the emotional and the rational elements of the personality. It is clear from his presentation that Erikson does not mean to limit the crises in the earlier stages only to the problems of orality, anality, or genitality. There are involved in each of the crises other factors—pain, muscular control of arms and legs, holding and letting go of things other than feces, and so on. To continue this broader approach in the later years seems equally reasonable, and even necessary for the healthy personality.

Trust and career. In his description of the initial stage in personality development Erikson describes the "trust versus mistrust" crisis in the following terms:

"Parents must not only have certain ways of guiding by prohibition and permission; they must also be able to represent to the child a deep, an almost somatic conviction that there is meaning to what they are doing. Ultimately, children become neurotic not from frustrations, but from the lack or loss of societal meaning in these frustrations." (Erikson, 1950, p. 222.)

The balance of forces in this dichotomy is seldom resolved once and for all, although conviction on one side or the other may grow stronger through reinforcement. This is probably especially true as one grows older and the philosophical bases of one's trust become more understood. In the early years, at least, any major change in the environment brings this crisis to the fore. The society of the family had meaning that was clear and easily comprehended. The society of friends developed meaning gradually. It too was small and comprehensible. The society of school incorporated the society of friends, broadening the bounds of friendship without changing its meaning. Gradually, as the individual advances through school its meanings become clearer and they begin to make an impact on the society of friends. This is a gradual evolution and is ordinarily, for the middle-class boy, not a problem. Public schools provide structure which reinforces familial meanings for the vast majority. Private schools do this for their own subcultural groups.

But the confrontation of the young person with the world of work is a major change in the environment. The world of work is a new world of meanings. Generally, family does not enter here, nor do peers.

For those who can perceive some meaning in the world of work there will probably be a renewed sense of trust. At this point it would seem that trust is a basic ingredient in the identity crisis leading to its resolution.

This interpretation may help to explain some of the underlying dynamics in the initial, trial, or exploratory stages of career development. Both the individual and society are striving to establish basic trust toward each other. Each is attempting to determine what meaning the other has for him and what meaning he has for the other. Failure occurs from a lack of meaning or an inadequately perceived conflict of meaning. Clearly perceived conflict will not ordinarily do damage, if both perceive the conflict. If the individual alone sees the conflict the industry probably will not suffer, but if the conflict is seen only by the industry and is not handled in a manner calculated to preserve the budding identity, then the business world can destroy for a long time the contribution which the person might make to the economy.

That counselors might shift the frames of reference and still maintain this basic trust would seem to follow from the position that this sense (and all others in the schema) is not achieved once and for all but is a constantly-to-be-maintained, dynamic thing. Thus if gradual shifts are supported and reinforced, it would seem that manpower needs could be filled from the pool of those who do have the talent or aptitude but not the values. This presumes the new value scale can be made desirable to them. Here we might consider the study of Bordin and Wilson (1953) in which they showed that course work had two effects on interest patterns—one, to cause some people who had low scores in the related interest area to shift out of course and obtain even lower scores in that area; the other, to cause other people whose scores in the related area were low, to take more courses in the field and to score higher on the interest scale.

This effect is probably also taking place in the students included in the National Merit Scholarship program. In a follow-up report on this program Forrest (1961) also notes "that recruiting efforts will fall short of success if they are limited to financial inducements alone." The pressure of money shortage can cause a temporary shift in career orientation but over the years the more basic meaning system begins to reject those meanings in the newly adopted career which are not consonant with it.

This approach, which emphasizes the way of life, may explain why the lower-class boy drops out of high school. His subculture gives no meaning to the frustration involved in further education. For the middle-class or upper-class boy, however, at this choice point, more education is given meaning by his cultural group. The decision to go to college is effortless, part of the accepted pattern, supported and reinforced by home, school, and adult environment in general.

It is, therefore, crucially important that the guidance counselor, in order to understand this aspect of the career development of his students, should have some acquaintance with sociological studies of subcultures and the interaction of these. In this matter we must be broadminded enough to recognize the value of all subcultures and their differing contributions to a pluralistic society. The motive for shifting some individuals may be the common good, but it must be done in a manner which preserves and does not destroy the individual. If the latter occurs, obviously the common good is not benefited.

In these terms the process of development would appear to be one of synthesis of newer elements with older meaning structures. The sense of identity, the sense of being all right, of being one's self may also be the basic reason for leaving a job and trying a new job. The person no longer has confidence in this meaning structure. He feels out of place. Hoppock (1960) found that, contrary to the press for stability as a key factor in personality integration, men who shifted jobs once, or even more often, ultimately found greater fulfillment in the new job.

It is clear from what we have been saying that more emphasis needs to be put on the unique factors in the individual and the job world. The concept of position (Tiedeman, O'Hara, and Matthews, 1958) rather than job or occupation should be considered because it is the unique constellations of factors that influence adjustment as well as the generic or common factors.

Thus one major hypothesis about career development deriving from the consideration of the trust-mistrust crisis is that *those people for whom the world of work has the greatest meaning consonant with their own previously developed meaning system will find the greatest satisfaction and success in their work.*

We have here fused two worlds—the unique world of the individual and the unique world of work. Vocational guidance should be the catalytic agent in this fusion.

This statement is not meant to imply that meaning systems are static things but that there must be an initial rapprochement which hopefully will grow and be productive for both the individual and for society. Since the economic society is unlikely to adapt itself in favor of the individual, and since individual adaptation has limits too, we have phrased the hypothesis in terms of what might be considered model career

development, recognizing that there will be shadings to either side.

Autonomy and career. In the Erikson schema the sense of autonomy entails the following notions: a sense of self control, environmental support for autonomous effort, which takes on two dimensions—prevention of premature effort and creation of opportunity for choice.

It would seem that the degree of autonomy granted in career development varies along a continuum. For example, there is some evidence for a type of independence which results in "letting the kid fend for himself." Upper middle-class parents encourage sports and competition in sons as preparation for the job world, while upper-class Harvard men reputedly become either lawyers or trustees. If this premature development of autonomy is highest in the lower classes, it may account for inability to defer its fulfillment in adolescence in school.

There is another dimension to the sense of autonomy which is probably more a function of personality "givens" than environmental formation. Its opposite might be considered to be dependence. There is some evidence to support the relevance of such a dimension in career development (White, 1952).

But there is more involved here than mere freedom in the sense of parents saying that their children can choose what they wish. That most parents in the United States do say this and mean it would seem to be true, but it would seem to be also true that there are environmental limitations on the range of one's freedom to choose an occupation which guidance counselors might well consider in the light of the explanation given here of autonomy. We are presently going through a period of increased emphasis on the wide range of choices available to our students, of increased realization of the large loss of manpower resulting from students making choices which are below the known level of their *aptitudes*. We adduce the inadequacy of their choices to a lack of information: (1) about the level of their aptitudes (and so we institute immense testing programs); and (2) about the opportunities available to people with such aptitudes (and so we have vocational information courses).

What would seem to be lacking in this plan is the development of specific environmental support for the autonomous effort necessary to complete the career. A generalized support from the dominant culture is not enough to fill up the vacuum of support or even overcome the opposition from the specific local environment in which the individual has roots. This is not a question of overt conscious opposition but of a way of life which does not provide the base of operations necessary for successful autonomous effort. If we then undertake to reduce our manpower loss by utilizing people from the less affluent economic groups we need to take great individual care of them to see that they are not overcome with shame resulting from premature effort. We need to be aware that their doubts about their careers may, on the surface, revolve around aptitude, but may perhaps stem more basically from an environmental uncertainty, the sense of aloneness, of being naked to my enemies,

even though the enemies are saying they are friends and are working for a fuller life for the individual.

For such people the problem is doubly difficult if we think that more direct support must be given to effect the change in career orientation, and yet for these people the earlier development of autonomy in their own milieu may be threatened by such support. It would almost seem in these cases that our success rate will be very low if we think in terms of the present generation, but a sustained effort over two generations might bear immense fruit. We expect that our need for talent will be as great in 1999 as it is in 1961.

Initiative and career. The sense of initiative emphasizes the idea that after a person discovers that he *is* a person he will now find out *what kind* of a person he is.

The process of finding out what kind of person one is continues throughout life. It is interesting to note here that there seems to be an anomaly in the position in that the kind of a person one is in the United States would seem to be predicated on the doing of things rather than the mere being, although it would also seem that this latter mode of establishing identity is at times recommended or even preferred. We who live in a future-doing oriented culture seem to alternate between acceptance and rejection of our way of life. The way of the weekend seems preferable to the way of the week. Perhaps the ideal order is that which the English have established, and we who would do away with weekends are the neurotic ones.

In relation to career development there are so many things one needs to know about one's self before one can learn what to do with them. As an example, take the question of intelligence. O'Hara and Tiedeman (1959) have shown that even for boys of above average intelligence this is a relatively difficult thing to estimate. Through the four years of a competitive college preparatory course the awareness of it increases but never reaches the level of interest awareness.

The problem of awareness is complicated by the fact that intelligence is usually measured by achievement, yet achievement is influenced by many other factors. Thus one can be prevented from taking intellectual initiative because one never really finds out that he is an intellectual.

It is clear that this type of analysis applies equally well to aptitudes other than intelligence, and to interests and values, as well as all the other factors that enter into career development.

The area of aptitude, particularly scholastic aptitude, is an extremely difficult one to handle in a public school. Cultural emphasis in these days of the cold war puts a premium on the bright boy. Not to be bright is generally to be looked down on in school. It is precisely at this point that the school loses its influence on the less bright unless there is provision within the curriculum for a sense of worth deriving from doing things that do not necessarily involve brightness. If the school is seen as a transmitter of the culture, counseling may not be so difficult.

For such less than bright students, considerations of the average quality of their aptitude are irrelevant. Other aspects of their personalities become more important to them, and other things than academic success. The sense of initiative needs to be encouraged outside of the curriculum and this in turn may redound through the personality in such a way that the average academic potential is fulfilled rather than lost. If such a person can say "It doesn't matter whether anyone else is interested in dual exhausts, I am, and it makes me happy to install them," then he is well on his way to solving this crisis.

Thus it would appear that for the average boy or girl to achieve a sense of unbroken initiative as a basis for a high and yet realistic sense of ambition and independence (Erikson, 1959, p. 75) a program of extracurricular activities would be required.

Aptitudes involve invidious comparisons made by adults and peers. Activities involving interests and values are not so oppressively laden with comparative concepts. They are then far less threatening, can be entered upon or relinquished without recrimination.

Industry and career. The environmental locus of this crisis is clearly the school. In this stage "I am what I learn," and learning can be conceived far too narrowly in our school systems. We are extremely aware of the need for developing a sense of being useful among our mentally retarded, but for boys and girls with IQ's of 80 to 100 who constitute about 40 percent of our school population we seem since Sputnik to be holding up the academic ideal. We can acknowledge that we have not challenged the talented without at the same time condemning the slower students to a built-in sense of inferiority. It would seem that educators have been very conscious of the immense numbers of boys and girls in this slower category and so have tended to organize life adjustment curriculums. For these people this may very well be the best possible type of education since it puts more emphasis on the kinds of things that they can do and will not foster a sense of inferiority for failure to know the square root of 144.

Careers for the talented will have different contours, motivations, and satisfactions from careers for the average or below average. If this is not clearly seen by counselors and educators, then in reality we are forcing a mode of activity on people in a manner that is quite undemocratic and will ultimately develop in vast numbers of people a sense of inferiority with dangerous potential.

That this position is valid would also seem to follow from the results of frequent surveys in the business world regarding the reasons for leaving. Seldom is lack of talent or ability the key factor. For the vast majority of the people it is crucially important to be well-adjusted.

For this sense (I am what I learn) the school system becomes the chief supporting environment. We have already noted how the home can reinforce the ideal of scholastic achievement, and if it does not, conflict may arise. It would seem necessary to restate this position in this context since to the lack of societal meaning may be added here the sense of inferiority. For the marginally above-average student who has a B and C record specific steps to make more proximate the achievement of the career goal may be necessary to overcome the growing sense of inferi-

ority. Here we find strong psychological support for the cooperative work-school programs which exist in some high schools and colleges.

Identity and career. All of these senses are focused toward the central sense of identity which forms at the climax of the biological growth and development, and is concomitant with the introduction of the person into the wider social world and the world of work. Entry to this latter world for the college-bound is delayed and thus ensues the culturally induced moratorium on earlier development of ego identity through career.

"In general it is primarily the inability to settle on an occupational identity which disturbs young people." (Erikson, 1959, p. 92.) Erikson, although only unobtrusively introducing the notion of occupational identity in the midst of this discussion of identity diffusion, seems to believe that the attainment of an occupational identity is crucial for the fulfillment of the definition of ego identity. Ego identity is defined as, "the accrued confidence that one's ability to maintain inner sameness and continuity (one's ego in the psychological sense) is matched by the sameness and continuity of one's meaning for others." (Erikson, 1959, p. 89.)

Through the preceding pages we have seen that the development of sameness and continuity takes place in the early years largely in the family and school environment. The entrance into the world of work is a relatively cold water shock. There is about it the quality of the unknown and untried. But it is more than mere exploration of a geographical place because "I am in the unknown and I am to become a part of it and it of me."

So it is utterly crucial that one should have help to know who one is as he comes to this central stage. This means that people should know that temporarily they may not be the same or continuous, that the process involves development and may involve great change. The cold water shock is nowhere more evident than in the home-school versus economic world meaning systems. Prior knowledge of the world of work must be introduced into the student's frame of reference. Successful adjustment to the job necessarily involves at least the preliminary formation of an ego identity. We can leave this to chance or we can save the economy and the state great manpower losses by introducing specific ways of facilitating the formation of identity.

"The integration now taking place in the form of ego identity is more than the sum of the childhood identifications." (Erikson, 1959, p. 89.) We have already noted some of the culturally induced identities in early life. Other identities are frequently experienced but we are unable to predict them. They come from myriad sources in the environment and with the advent of mass communication the possibility of a farm boy identifying with an oceanographer from Woods Hole is no longer remote.

How the early identifications are integrated into the new identity has received little study except from the pathological point of view. It would appear that the vocational aspect is crucial for successful integration. This approach to personality and careers puts great emphasis on sincere and continuous support and approval from society. To understand truly the interaction we need a matrix of measures of (1) the culture, (2) the boy's perception of the culture, (3) his perception of himself in the culture (this latter measure ought ideally to be a developmental record), (4) perceptions of the boy by key people, (5) "objective" measures of the boy. Our initial attempt to do this was in the context of the nursing school (Kibrick and Tiedeman, 1961). The nursing school was taken as a subculture of its own, with its own positions and meaning systems.

The full impact of the social world and its approval or disapproval is more sweepingly felt in the period of the identity crisis since here one experiences in a much larger measure freedom of choice with the consequences falling on the individual's shoulders rather than on those of parents or teachers. "I can no longer blame anyone else except myself. Now those who can blame become important to me." Decisions leading to success are utterly necessary.

Intimacy and distantiation and career. We shall mention here only the concept of distantiation—"the readiness to repudiate, to isolate, and if necessary, to destroy those forces and people whose essence seems dangerous to one's own." (Erikson, 1959, p. 95.) In career development terms this would clearly underlie the next stage which research shows exists in career—a horizontal mobility involving several job changes. These are now seen as necessary for the preservation of the budding identity.

It is necessary also to distinguish between those

forces that are truly dangerous to one's essence and those that are apparently so but are in reality the most life-giving modalities . . . "unless the seed, falling into the ground, die, itself remains alone."

The earlier stages of this crisis may be seen in the ability or inability to make negative decisions about interests and values. This point has been made by Tyler (1959). This is a clear case in which negative limits are not only therapeutic but seminal and productive.

Generativity versus stagnation. "Generativity is primarily the interest in establishing and guiding the next generation." (Erikson, 1959, p. 97.) If this concept is applied to the world of work, particularly by the captains of industry, then work takes on a far deeper meaning than the externals of money and status can give it. Creativity puts the emphasis on the newness of the thing. Productivity puts emphasis on the action and the amount of both things and money. Certainly both of these emphases are fulfilling, but they need to be joined to the generational emphasis for the fulfillment of the man of wisdom. Thus, the creative man in the world of work is the inventor or researcher; the productive man is the general manager; but the chairman of the board ought to be a man of wisdom who will control both of these men and be able to paraphrase in a generational context, "What is good for John Doe is good for General Motors." Perhaps this conception comes only in the fullness of age when one sees sons and grandsons entering the world of work.

Integrity versus despair. The position enunciated above leads us to a new application of *noblesse oblige.* The life style of the career man that finds its fulfillment in competition alone rather than in generativity will lead our country into bankruptcy. If the hierarchy of need theory is true (Maslow, 1954), then the new lords of the economic world should be especially capable of this new nobility since they have passed beyond the level of other needs. The generous man will dedicate his work, his company, to his culture, to generations yet unborn, and find in this dedication a climactic integrity akin to the mutuality of love.

In this section, then, we have attempted to adumbrate some of the successive differentiations and integrations of personality that undergird successful career development. Some of the diverse modes which differentiation and integration may take are evident in the cases and in the suggested applications for guidance practice. We see these only as first steps toward a consistent theory.

Section IV. Time and occupation: A frame for career development

Recapitulation

We have so far set forth the premise that a person more or less continuously develops an attitude or posture toward himself and his situation in life. This attitude toward self-in-situation is ego identity. Such attitudes are one source of intentions which are guides of action. Work is one of the accomplishments of human action. Hence, the locus of career development is in this presumably continuously differentiating ego-identity.

The evolving ego-identity therefore creates a number of premises which frame an attitude about one's self in one's world. We may speak of this emerging psychological life-space as a person's cognitive map of himself in the world. The elements of the cognitive map are within a person's awareness. The anger, joy, certainty, fear, doubt, envy, shame, and guilt surrounding many of the premises of this cognitive map are not necessarily fully appreciated by the person, however. These emotional concomitants of premises are not easy to know or to control. Usually we merely help a person to see them a little for himself. Nevertheless, they are a necessary aspect of a theory of career development.

Attitudes form around experience. Experience results from activity and reflection upon one's condition before, during, and after the activity. It takes time to act and to think. It is difficult to consider or undertake two or more things simultaneously because the mometary span of human attention is finite and small. These aspects of the human condition require the rational person to fit his career into life. Hence time is important to career development.

Let us consider this matter of time limitation of career a little more. In general, occupation is discussed as work and as if the time in which work is practiced was boundless. Obviously, neither of these conditions is a necessary one. In its root meaning occupation includes thinking, sitting, playing, a myriad of activities which may claim attention. Furthermore, the practice of one activity does preclude the practice of another, to some extent at least; the day, the week, the year, the life are each finite. To study the occupancy of time therefore is to study the seizure of time by the sundry activities of living possible throughout a lifetime. With some people, observable apportionment of time to activity may be utterly capricious; such people are completely responsive to the contingencies of living. Other people may treasure time more; for them time occupancy is to be planned, to have a desired yield. The subject of time occupancy offers a means then of organizing the study of career development as an analysis of the investment of time so that the yield to the individual is optimum.

Obviously, the variety of combinations of activity and awareness that may occupy attention in a particular period of time is extensive. Furthermore, patterns of time occupancy change with age. Physical and mental capacities inflict their mark upon the pattern. Intent, plan, and organization of self further individualize time occupancy. Kinds of activities and awareness lend further complexity to the variety of patterns. These and other variations will be considered as we progress.

The primary purpose of our exploration is to offer a view of occupation with work within an evolving pattern of modes with which time is occupied by activity and awareness. Our primary hope is that the study of career development might thereby become a more consistent part of the study of personal development. A logical framework is needed within which such consistency may emerge.

The biological imprint upon time occupancy

The biological requirements for maintaining life necessarily pre-empt attention and activity in a variety of ways. Among these requirements is the important demand for sleep and relaxation. The demand for sleep is exceptionally heavy in infancy. The demand declines throughout childhood and adolescence and reaches a minimal stage in the young adult. In late adulthood and old age the demand for replenishment of the bodily systems again becomes heavier but probably does not reach the level inflicted upon the infant. Sleep does inflict a heavy toll upon time for work in infancy and old age, however.

The evidence concerning the biological necessity of relaxation is not clear. If sufficient periods of sleep are provided regularly life continues despite an absence of other relaxation. Even such strict regimens must provide some variety in activity and thought, however. Also, efficiency is known to suffer if a change of pace is not permitted. Attention cannot be sustained efficiently over any extended period of time. Even in the dire condition of war, society makes formal allowance for relaxation. Certainly there is some taking up of occupation with relaxation by occupation with work during war. The latter is not permitted entirely to supersede the former, however.

Our argument is not lost if relaxation is not considered a biological demand. As we will suggest later, we are interested in the biological, personal, social identity as player. In this context we will deal not merely with the mere demand for relaxation; we will deal also with learned modes and demands for relaxation. Momentarily, we note here merely the expectation of considerable play held before the child and the retired worker and the opportunity for entertainment offered the adolescent and adult. The young adult is not expected to play much as he undertakes the serious problem of establishing himself. Nevertheless, a considerable portion of occupation throughout the life cycle is with relaxation and this portion is likely to increase with increasing automation. In passing, we also note that play and entertainment are the socially accepted means of attaining a sexual identity in childhood and adulthood and thus of responding to the sexual demand upon one's destiny.

In addition to the sleep and relaxation that are necessary for regularly replenishing one's capability to think and to do, regular ingestion and elimination of solids and liquids are needed. These imperatives may pre-empt slightly more time in the infant life than thereafter. Perhaps the child gives the least attention to the satisfaction of these needs, but one of his parents must spend quite a bit of time with this occupation. The demand seems to occupy two to three hours per day for a considerable span of the life.

Maslow's safety needs (1954) are largely fulfilled for the infant by his elders. As the child becomes more aware of these requirements for maintaining life he seemingly devotes more time to them. In general, these needs do not occupy much time, however, until the young adult assumes responsibility for his own keep. Somewhat earlier the adolescent is supposed to learn of law and order and its contribution

Figure 2: Biological pre-emption of time occupancy

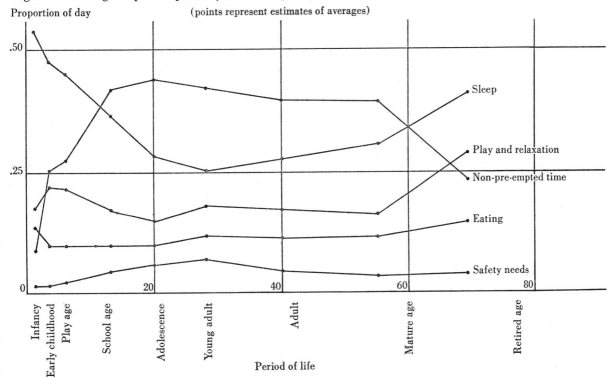

to his safety if he maintains law. At this period, too, the adolescent is wrestling with specification of his identity and is thereby faced with the dilemma of security of his personal-social "position" and all the concomitant issues of that question. Thus, safety needs rise in adolescence and stay at a peak, particularly for the male, throughout his adult life. An elder is excused from some participation in security maintenance. Safety needs are difficult to chart because they are indefinite. Despite this difficulty, however, we have roughly estimated them in Figure 2 because they are a part of the time-occupancy situation we are trying to comprehend.

The sociocultural imprint upon time occupancy

Cultural and social expectations, as well as the aforementioned biological condition of man, also inscribe a lasting imprint upon the developing pattern of time occupancy. Prime among these cultural expectations are those defining the structure of a society.

When the behavior of a party requires that another party to a meeting respond to it, we say that interaction occurs. As noted earlier, interaction does not necessarily occur in every meeting of two people. Interaction occurs only when there is expectation on the part of one member of the meeting that the other member should respond to him. There is structure-in-interaction when the pre-empting response of the originator and the reply of the respondent pattern in some way (Hemphill, 1958). Patterning or reproducibility is a product of teaching, habit, custom, regulation, law, and belief.

Structure-in-interaction can make interaction more efficient. The traffic light at a street corner is an example; selective admission to college, another. Behavior is reasonably predictable when a structure exists in interaction. Communication can then occur more effectively. Behavior is also practiced when a structure exists in interaction. The expected transaction can then transpire in a shorter period of time than would otherwise be required.

The premises of a structure-in-interaction are ordinarily considered to be relatively permanent. This is so because the premises of structure-in-interaction are largely anchored in the system of values and attitudes of each citizen. They reflect his belief. Such cultural imperatives are mostly premises of some meaning; they are "charged"; they are the ideas which please or anger us. America is "the land of the free and the home of the brave," for example. Grown men earn their own keep and pay taxes, to cite another example. The premises of structures-in-interaction are the premises with which we live in comfort, then; they protect our freedom by ordering the outside world so that we know what to expect; they are a part of the psychology of containment upon which each of us relies in organizing himself.

It is necessary that each person have a way to relate himself to each of the demands which his body, environment, and society place upon him. Obviously, full examination of each of the myriad of such demands is impossible as the demand occurs. Furthermore, the demands are so numerous that full examination beforehand or afterwards is also impractical.

We do develop simplifying schemes for handling demands as a result. What we are taught; what we are required to do; what we develop as structures-in-interaction; all such habits, and governing concepts are a part of the orientation of a person to his situation. It seems reasonable to designate these mechanisms for the control of situation as principles of containment. Defenses are principles of containment but not all principles of containment need be considered defensive. Principles of containment are merely means of simplification, of classification, of ordering. It is useful to know the organization of these principles of containment because they largely govern the matters to which a person attends.

As adults mature they sometimes discover that the premises of structures-in-interaction are not as certain as they were led to believe as youths. Some aspects of structure-in-interaction are subject to the continual interpretation of those appointed to administer the task associated with the charter of those premises. The President of the United States does act upon *his* interpretation of the Constitution and the laws of the land after all. Science is *not* what I learned twenty years ago. Railways are *not* a necessary part of the system of transport of passengers. Structural premises are a part of the system of beliefs of a land then, but are continually subject to the interpretation of the living citizenry whenever such interpretations must be made or can be made. Therefore, there is some doubt or uncertainty that must be attributed to the so-called norms or cultural imperatives which are some of the structural premises.

Furthermore, some structural premises are subject to learning and to re-education.

We are not capable of entering into a full presentation of the premises of the structures-in-interaction of American society. Therefore, we shall try to note only those premises seemingly of relevance to occupation and identity although, even in this more circumscribed realm, our own knowledge is presently still very limited.

The key to "becoming" in American culture is the assumption of personal responsibility or independence (Super, 1959). Otherwise one doesn't "become"; one "is." The wish to be independent is reasonably viable in everyone. In the United States, however, the requirement of independence is early placed before the child. Ordinarily the child is reared in a mother-father household and does not share the mother's bed long, if at all. Frequently, the child is soon required to sleep in a room by itself. The child is weaned early, taught to feed himself as soon as he is capable of doing so, and is early expected to control excretion. He is taught to dress himself as he becomes capable of it. School soon follows upon these requirements. Work is expected early in life and the parents technically fulfill their obligations as their children marry soon after the start of independent work. Independence seemingly has taken its course but an ultimate task remains for which each new family must strive as it in turn starts a new generation; the elders of each family in America are expected to provide for their own independence when they are no longer permitted to work and must retire.

The several cultural milestones in the evolution of independent status which are staged in Figure 3 are of sufficient importance to be associated with a definite role in the society. Roles of relevance to the study of career development are: (1) the sex role, including the relevant role in one's own family; (2) student-worker; (3) citizen; and (4) class. Each of the roles has a prescribed set of rights and obligations within the structure of the society. Each person must learn of the customs of his land as he grows up. These customs prescribe one's identity to a considerable degree, of course, but prescription is not necessarily bad. Structures-in-interaction that can be relied upon are a necessary adjunct of freedom.

The effects of these pressures for independence are further channeled through a sequence of interper-

Figure 3: The staging of expectations for independence

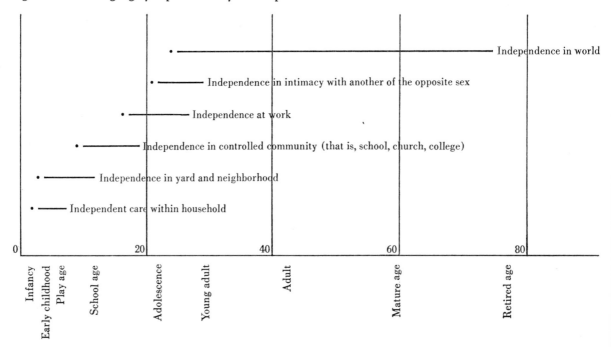

sonal problems. These interpersonal problems are another aspect of the human condition which leaves its imprint upon the evolving ego-identity.

The effects of the resolutions of these interpersonal problems upon personality and career have been specified in the previous section after the manner of Erikson (1959). Since in this section we are interested in specifically denoting the life context of the

Figure 4: The staging of the forms of identity

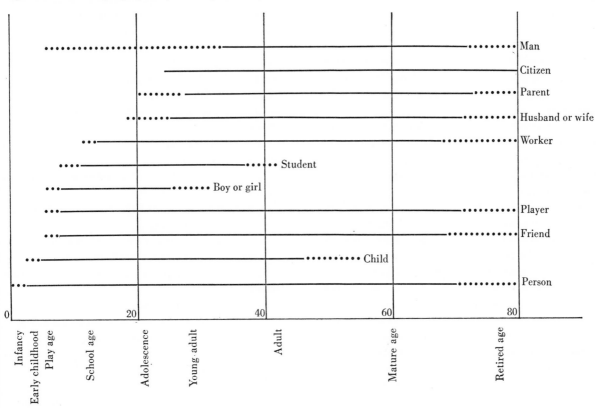

career problem, we portray here the interpersonal problem of identity formation against the backdrop of time (see Figure 4).

The problem of identity formation is to integrate the press for independence within the general roles of the society as these become imperative as interpersonal problems. The general problem of identity requires differentiation and later integration of numerous structures-in-interaction as a result. Many of the ensuing crises are "open" for a considerable period. Some are never faced. Some are faced without resolution of an earlier problem. These differences create some of the variety we observe in adult character.

The expectations associated with each of the several roles noted above vary with the subculture with which a person identifies. Religion, ethnic origin, and socioeconomic position of a family each leaves its stamp upon the expectations a person learns for a role. The Christian Scientist is supposed to profess no role for the doctor. The German is likely to favor a different view of the worker role than does the Spaniard. The laborer is likely to transmit a view of class different from that transmitted by the Boston Brahmin. Research on social influence on job perception (Grunes, 1956) illustrates this point.

Finally, we note that the evolving cognitive map of relevance for career development is further differentiated by the staging of study and work permitted in this country. The staging of study and work gives rise to a series of choices. We shall refer to the options available in school and work as positions. We

do so because we seek a general word at this time which will permit articulation with the language of sociology. Position choices are another means of further differentiating structures-in-interaction.

Position choices can occur at any instant subsequent to attainment of legal working age and prior to forced retirement from a position. There are times when position choice *must* occur and other times when it *can* occur. In the first case the situation is defined externally and in the second, internally. The forces of relevance to the process of position choice are related to the discontinuities discussed by Hottel (1955, pp. 4-5, 8, 20, 31). The vocationally relevant position choices inherent in these several discontinuities include:

1. Selection of part-time employment while in school and afterwards;

2. Selection of subjects to be taken in junior high school;

3. Selection of subjects to be taken in high school;

4. Selection of a college;

5. Selection of a program of study in college;

6. Selection of a graduate school;

7. Selection of a program of study in graduate school;

8. Selection of an Armed Service;

9. Selection of a specialty in an Armed Service;

10. Selection of first full-time position;

11. Selection of another position when dissatisfaction arises over a former position; and

12. Retirement.

We have listed above only the obvious discontinuities which make choice and subsequent limitation of life chances a necessity. Our previous discussion of identity as it evolves in the acquisition of roles appropriate for solution of the interpersonal problems of the life condition suggests that choices of positions of a nonoccupational nature are also an important matter. We have not wished to specify these at this time although Havighurst's (1953) developmental tasks continue to capture our interest.

Each of the discontinuities we have noted above has a fairly definite age at which it begins. The age of termination is indefinite in most instances when the entire populace is considered. Nevertheless, it is useful to give a time perspective to these discontinuities and we therefore present a tentative time schedule in Figure 5.

Three types of suggestions with regard to time are indicated in Figure 5. One suggestion designates ages at which the problem must be considered. The line is solid (_____) in these time periods. The broken line (- - - - -) indicates a period when the problem could and may exist. This period should be included with the periods of the solid line when possible. Dotted lines (. . . . .) indicate periods when the problem could exist but probably does not. Probably, little would be lost if these periods were excluded from consideration.

The staging of both bodily and social development each places a heavy imprint upon the evolution of ego-identity. These stages therefore represent necessary limits upon a theory of career development.

Figure 5: Staging of study and work discontinuities

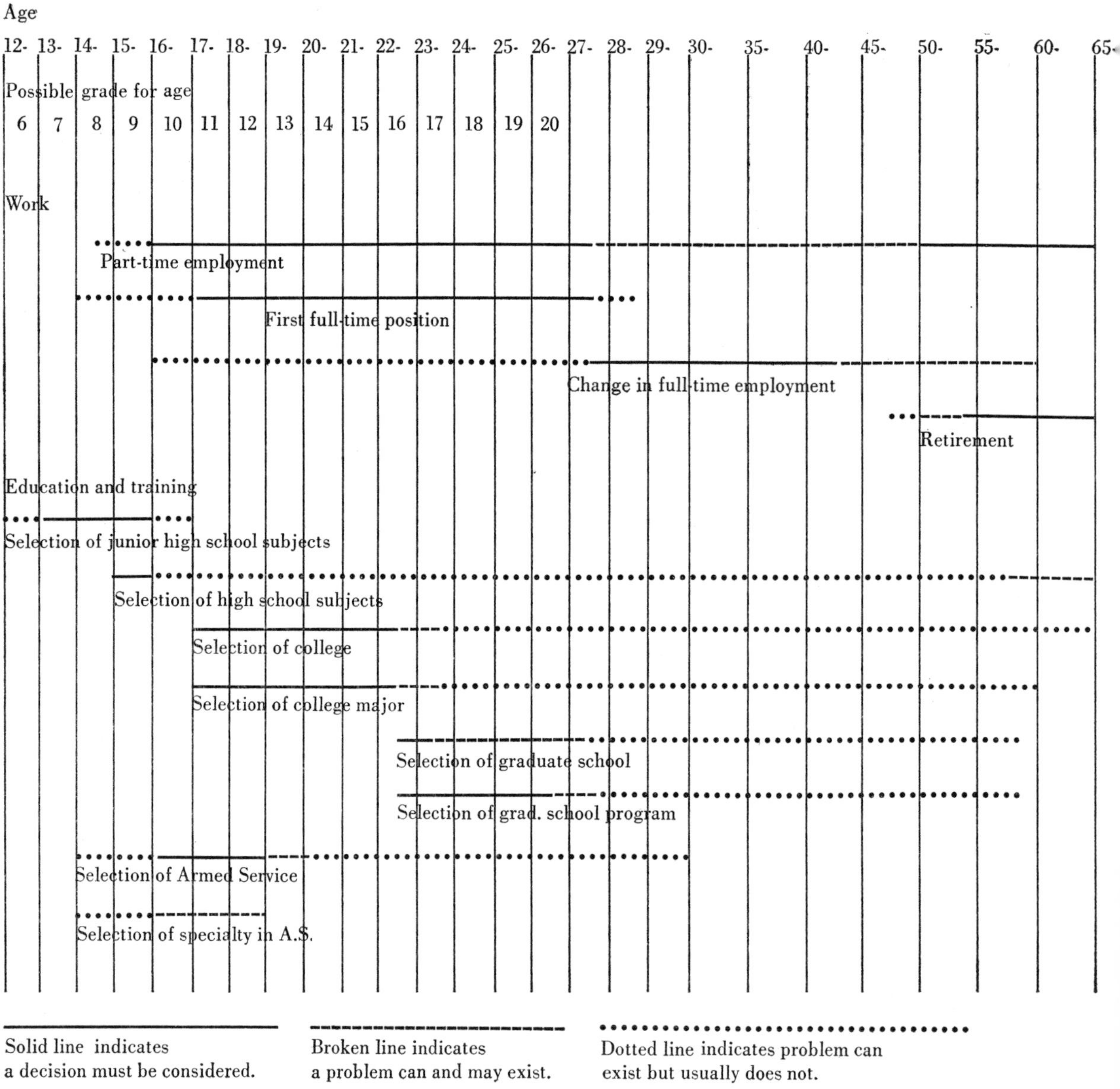

Age

12-	13-	14-	15-	16-	17-	18-	19-	20-	21-	22-	23-	24-	25-	26-	27-	28-	29-	30-	35-	40-	45-	50-	55-	60-	65-

Possible grade for age

6	7	8	9	10	11	12	13	14	15	16	17	18	19	20

Work

Part-time employment

First full-time position

Change in full-time employment

Retirement

Education and training

Selection of junior high school subjects

Selection of high school subjects

Selection of college

Selection of college major

Selection of graduate school

Selection of grad. school program

Selection of Armed Service

Selection of specialty in A.S.

Solid line indicates a decision must be considered.

Broken line indicates a problem can and may exist.

Dotted line indicates problem can exist but usually does not.

Section V. Observation and career: An assessment of, and some suggestions for, research in career development

Career and the work history

We have demonstrated the powerful way in which a paradigm of differentiation and integration organizes information from the realms of vocational choice and personality. Information from these realms proved readily accessible in the conversations with Bob, Paul, Steve, and Val. The realms of vocational choice and of personality span the realms of career.

In a later section we completely specified our paradigm of differentiation and integration and related the concept of career to it. The ensuing section outlined the biological and cultural imperatives which give definition to the life situation and both impel and bound the development of career. In the present section we shall consider several problems for empiric investigation as they are suggested by our concepts. We shall also note relevant research completed elsewhere but our primary purpose here is to offer a review of research within our purview. Such a review has not been available heretofore.

The primary product of career development is the work history. The salient structural characteristics of the work history are: (1) the kinds of positions a person holds in the course of his life; (2) the se-

quence of those positions; and (3) the duration of the intervals between positions (Tiedeman, 1961). The impetus for change is also of considerable import in the relation of career to the work history. Did the initiative for change rest with the person or with those in control of opportunity? If the initiative rested with the person, what was the basis of the change? If the initiative rested with others, what personal satisfaction arose from the ensuing effort of a person to relocate himself?

The object of empiric study in career development is to increase our power to control relevant aspects of the work history. The attainment of this purpose requires specification of the relation of career to the work history. This specification must be open to empiric investigation.

We shall initiate specification of the relation of career and the work history in this section. In doing so we shall consider: (1) the demand that our complex theory places upon the representation of the work history whether noted as a matter of record or predicted as a matter of an evolving science of career development; and (2) the problem of specifying the input necessary for anticipation of work histories. In this latter instance we shall discuss: (1) the origins of goals; (2) the process of valuing vocational goals; (3) opportunity and position choice; (4) eligibility and position choice; (5) the prediction of position choice; (6) self, identity, and career; and (7) a psychosocial theory of career.

A model for representing the work history

A work history may consist of: (1) periods of un-employment; (2) periods of holidays, or vacations, or both; and (3) periods of employment in which a person (a) may hold one position; or (b) hold two or more positions simultaneously. In either of those last two instances continuation is assured over a standard small interval until some event occurs which discontinues the person's activity in the position. A complex theory of career development must relate career to work history with allowance for all of these contingencies. This requires complex control upon the writing of the record of the work history whether this record be of past events or the prediction of future events. The concept of a holding relay of an accounting machine offers such possibility.

Suppose we imagine that a relay, one to a row, is either open or closed as the bank of relays is controlled in time. If a relay is open, a person is occupying the position corresponding to the relay; if closed, the person does not occupy the position. Each relay operates independently of all others. Each relay may be wired so that, once open, a subsidiary impulse continuously reactivates the control of the relay so as to keep the relay open. Such wiring is referred to as a holding relay. By means of the concept of holding relay we may encompass all that we need to consider in the problem of choosing positions; namely, a system where any set of relays may be activated at a particular instant, but, when once activated, remains activated continuously until de-activated.

Thus the holding relay analogy allows for continuity within a system where this continuity is continuously re-examined throughout any interval of time that one wishes to create—a year, a month, a week, a day, or less.

In order to illustrate our analogy, let us consider the type of record our bank of relays would create if they controlled an output mechanism which pressed a pen to paper traveling continuously under the pens when a relay was open and retracted the pen from the paper when the relay was closed. Suppose further that our interval of reconsideration of activity were a day. A person who occupied the position of accountant for company X and advised clients with regard to their Federal Income Tax when he could, would have a record which showed a line corresponding to the position, accountant of company X, which would be interrupted only by holidays and vacations, and a simultaneous line corresponding to the position of tax consultant, which would be absent during much of the record for a year but would be an intermittent line with dashes of varying size for the period from January through April.

On the other hand, the career record of a married woman with children who sold subscriptions to a magazine by telephoning potential prospects might show an intermittent line concentrated in the period prior to the Christmas holidays. We expect this line to be interrupted by illness, serious illness of her children, husband, or hers, the vacations of her children or of her husband, preparation for a party or the arrival of company, success which made her earnings more than she wanted, discouragement of repeated refusal, or examination of the utilization of her leisure. If the husband were to take a new position in a different location, the career line of this woman might be interrupted only by the time necessary for moving and settling. This is a position she could occupy in several locations. Personal illness, relocation, or saturation of desire are accepted as reasons for the interruption of the career line of the man. Illness of wife and children over an extended period, housekeeping, vacation of the wife or children, and discouragement are not accepted as reasons for interruption of the career line of the man. The wife is ordinarily expected to subordinate her career to that of the husband, not vice versa. The husband is usually expected to subordinate the life of his family and of himself to the demands of his position so long as this is financially necessary and so long as the demands of the position do not exceed rather wide boundaries of safety and personal satisfaction.

In order to encompass the full range of opportunity for position occupancy in this country it is necessary that the bank of position relays of our career recorder include the positions corresponding to: (1) full-time employment; (2) part-time employment; (3) self-employment; (4) private investment management; and (5) artistry pursued for commercial purposes.

Origins of goals

The above model merely offers a means of recording the work history. It does not speak to the creation of a work history. We speak to this problem here and in the remainder of this paper.

The above machine model for the intermittent representations of the result of vocational decisions must be guided by a system possessing the characteristics of the paradigm of differentiation and integration we have noted in Section III. A primary problem in that paradigm is the anticipation of the goals likely to be under consideration at a moment of interest.

Where do vocational goals originate? The answer is not well-known. For years vocational psychologists have relied upon interests and values (for example, Strong, 1955) to detect inclinations toward vocational goals. Roe (1956) recently raised questions about the origins of such interests. Roe's present research effort (1961) is devoted to the study of a theory postulating dependence of occupational pursuits on parental control of the subject as a child. Although some of her results are as expected, many are not. Furthermore, an earlier study of Hagen (1960) failed to unearth the relationships predicated in Roe's theory (1957) among a set of retrospective reports on early family atmosphere. This line of research needs further work because it is extremely important for a theory of career development.

Tyler (1951) has made more specific investigations of the interests of children and observed a sex-typing of occupations in the early grades of elementary school. These observations can be heard in the taped interviews on vocational development which several of our students have prepared (Levine, 1959; Newman, 1959).

The most definitive indications of the origins of vocational goals are to be found in studies of occupational inheritance (for example, Jensen and Kirchner, 1955). The level of job a son takes very frequently coincides with that of his father. The level of education to which a child aspires is intimately linked with the socioeconomic level of his family (for example, Shea, 1960). McArthur proposes (personal communication) that this dependence is further mediated by the attitude of a child toward his parents. Pandit (Tiedeman and Pandit, 1958) demonstrated that the level of occupational aspiration also depends on the degree of congruity of an adolescent's evaluations of himself and those he attributes to others, relevant to his situation. Herriott (1961) showed high correlation between educational aspiration and the definition of expectation and support an adolescent offers about his life situation.

We have also been involved in a number of studies which attempted to predict educational and occupational choices. These studies are summarized in the later subsection, "The Prediction of Position Choice."

The process of valuing vocational goals

Vocational membership is related to values (Allport, Vernon, Lindzey, 1960; Rosenberg, 1957). Despite the quantity of these studies, however, the process of valuing in relation to vocational goals has largely escaped attention. It is true that the *Study of Values* (Allport, Vernon, and Lindzey, 1960) forces valuing by forcing choice. Only the resulting order is considered, however; the basis of choice is not considered. Tyler (1961) recently called our attention to the important data resident in denotation of the basis of choice. Her study was of choosing in relation to vocational alternatives, too. Many value studies deliberately avoid the vocational idiom. On the other hand, interest studies are largely set in the vocational idiom. Is the difference not merely in the concepts that one is required to order? Do not both really portray the result of ordering phenomena of relevance to one's life situation? We think so.

Opportunity and position choice

A choice implies the availability of at least two alternatives. Position choice has a similar implication. A choice is forced, however, when, while occupying one position, a person is offered others. A person's decision in this circumstance depends heavily upon whether the person has found an opportunity or had an offer made to him.

Position choice is also created when the person is currently unemployed and is offered a position. In these circumstances, choice may be only a take-it-or-leave-it proposition if only one position is available. If two or more positions are available simultaneously choice is more likely to provide satisfaction.

The four circumstances of position choice which must be differentiated are indicated in Figure 6. This figure suggests that predisposition of the person will be toward the offer in three of the four cases.

Figure 6: *Expected predispositions of a person in several circumstances of position choice*

Person			Offer	
			Sought	*Tendered*
	Employed	{	Predisposition toward offer	Predisposition indeterminate
	Unemployed	{	Predisposition toward offer	Some predisposition toward offer

Even when the initiative is with another, we feel that, in probability, a person is predisposed toward the offer even though we have recorded the predisposition as indeterminate. We have this feeling because another person is unlikely to make a random offer. Rather that person is likely to aim his offer at someone who he feels will see a chance for advancement in the offer and who will therefore take it. Thus in all four circumstances we hypothesize a predisposition toward change of present position which should be considered in predicting position choice provided this information is known when a prediction is made. The likelihood associated with the several alternatives varies in as yet unspecified ways, of course.

Among men and single women, we feel that the relative order of this predisposition is:

1. Person unemployed with initiative for offer his.

2. Person employed with initiative for offer his.

3. Person unemployed with initiative for offer that of another.

4. Person employed with initiative for offer that of another.

As we have suggested, we feel that the fourth predisposition is a weak one and probably the difference in predisposition between the third and fourth ranks is much greater than the difference between the other two adjacent pairs of ranks. When unemployed, the press for work is strong in men. When dissatisfied, the press for change of work is strong in men. When neither unemployed nor dissatisfied, the press for change is weak.

Among married women, the ranks of these predispositions are probably altered somewhat. We feel that the predispositions may rank in this order:

1. Person employed with initiative for offer hers.

2. Person unemployed with initiative for offer hers.

3. Person employed with initiative for offer that of another.

4. Person unemployed with initiative for offer that of another.

We have several reasons for this supposition, no one of which has been verified. We feel that, because the married woman ordinarily considers herself a secondary breadwinner, unemployment is less of a threat. Consequently, we feel that an unemployed married woman will be fairly discriminating about offers and will not be inclined to accept just any offer she manages to turn up. The employed married woman, on the other hand, is likely to seek change in position only when the circumstances of the new position are pretty well understood by her and consequently the predisposition toward the offer will be greatest in this case. When the initiative for an offer is not hers, the married woman is more likely to accept the offer if employed than if unemployed. We hold this position because, when trying to convince an unemployed woman that she should work for him, an employer must first convince her that she should work. This task is usually unnecessary when a woman is already employed. In the case of married women, we feel that the difference in predisposition toward the offer is larger between the ranks 2 and 3 than between the other two adjacent pairs of ranks.

Our suppositions concerning these predispositions, their order, their magnitude, and the differences between their order for men and single women as contrasted with married women could, of course, be interesting subjects of investigations. Some of the conditions which create differential orderings or changes in magnitudes of the predispositions could also be examined.

So far, however, we have limited our discussion to the influence on position choice of a known available opportunity. The study of position choice in relation to opportunity includes subjects in addition to this one of course. We are interested in the demand for occupants of different positions at particular times in the future. We are also interested that, when opportunity exists, its availability is shared by many interested parties.

Although it is not possible to specify fully the positions that will exist at a future time, the present condition in this regard is ordinarily a good guide for several years. There are several matters in this use of the status quo to specify the future condition of positions that are worthy of note, namely:

1. *There is considerable variation of positions within jobs.* A company specifies its needs in terms of a job. So many persons are needed to fill this job. A job may be carefully described in the employment office in terms of duties and responsibilities.

We would define position as involving the unique reality of this job, the internal perceptions of it by its holder as well as by the holder's bosses, equals, and subordinates. This uniqueness is what ultimately makes for job satisfaction and successful performance. It follows from this that personnel officers need to be as aware of the personalities involved as of the duties and responsibilities. Recognition of this distinction between job and position is crucial for all those engaged in the world of work. The reality testing process of implementation and adjustment is primarily centered around the position, if one has been trained successfully for the job. If training has not preceded the hiring then the reality testing may be concerned with the duties and responsibilities of the job as well as the unique relationships involved.

As long as an employee continues to satisfy the work demands of his employer, the employee or his supervisor may redefine the employee's position from time to time without changing the employee's job. This fact further complicates exhaustive specification of available positions at a future time. The flow of work is executed by people and most generally requires their interaction in attacking the product to be processed. An employee interested in expediting the flow of work may one day or one hour discharge one set of responsibilities and another day or hour a different set of responsibilities. Consider for example the clerk who one day processes time slips, the next day employment applications, and a third day teaches a new employee how to process both kinds of records. If we were to focus upon the discharge of the several responsibilities of a position, we believe that we could consider many of the problems of satisfaction with work. Many studies could be undertaken on the problems of opportunity for self-introduction of new responsibilities, or opportunity for variation of the sequence and pace of discharge of responsibilities, and of effect of particular people who occupy positions with which a particular employee must interact in the discharge of his responsibilities.

2. *Jobs change from time to time.* As the economy changes so do industries, occupations, and jobs. These changes influence the particular patterns of responsibilities that define positions. If we were to focus upon functional responsibilities of positions perhaps the influence of these variations can be minimized. The Armed Forces, for instance, have reported success in anticipating the maintenance of electronic equipment as it became operational from the analysis of functional operations on only the prototypes available during development of the operational model. Although the functional responsibilities may pattern in different ways in new jobs, perhaps there are greater invariances in the functional responsibilities themselves than we realize and hence of the immutability and availability of already developed skills.

3. *Knowledge, perception, and valuations of positions vary with the person choosing a position.* With our focus on career development, we presume that the purposes of the study of positions will be to predict choice and continuation in the position chosen. The knowledge a person has of the alternatives available, and his perception and valuation of the pattern of obligations of the position and of the life the position enables, will influence his choice and continuation in the position. Hence the study of positions should be undertaken in relation to the knowledge, perceptions, and valuations of those who are to choose and work in a position. Otherwise the classification of positions achieved may be irrelevant to the problem of choice and continuation and, as a result, be unpredictable. The ultimate classification must, of course, be specified independent of the person choosing or else no prediction is possible. We think, however, that predictions will be improved if proper attention is given to the internal frame of reference of the one who is to choose.

Blau, Gustad, Jessor, Parnes, and Wilcock (1956) have presented a framework for perceiving occupational choice which is not too different from the concept we have just described. In addition, Hilton (1962) has developed a flow chart of career decision-making with the concept of cognitive dissonance at its core. The Hilton model is quite consistent with the general problem being developed here. We agree that the capacity to predict a career record in the study of career development requires a model with the fluidity of the multiple relays, operating simultaneously, and controlled by holding relays which we have advanced. This model focuses attention squarely upon the work history as the ultimate interest of career development. Within the concepts of our model, the problem of predicting career development may be simply described as that of predicting the sequence and duration of operation of the relays that are controlled simultaneously, singly, or intermittently to trace out the career of a person.

Eligibility and position choice

A person must seem to qualify for a position before he is offered the position. As Blau and others (1956) have pointed out, position prerequisites are of two kinds, functional and nonfunctional. The functional requirements are most frequently written out; the nonfunctional requirements are most frequently found out through experience in seeking a position.

Functional prerequisites result from analyses of positions and from study of the antecedents of incumbents of positions in relation to their performance in the position. Our knowledge of functional prerequisites is of six different kinds: (1) relevant antecedents; (2) minimum requirements; (3) education; (4) apprenticeship; (5) experience; and (6) legal specifications.

Identification of relevant antecedents. The psychologist has largely been content merely to identify those antecedents required in a specific job. There are few efforts to offer empiric justification of minimum requirements for various jobs. Dorcus and Jones (1950) have abstracted many studies identifying antecedents relevant to success on a job. Super treats this material systematically both in his *Appraising Vocational Fitness* (1949) and in his *The Psychology of Careers* (1957, pp. 198-280). The latter treatment is most relevant because it is organized by the theme of vocational development. Thorndike and Hagen (1959) recently reported an extensive predictive study of this nature for many occupational areas.

Minimum requirements. The specification of minimum requirements for entry into work is for the most part limited to the considered opinions of experienced persons (for example, Paterson, Gerken, and Hahn, 1953; U. S. Department of Labor, 1956). Verification of these propositions is a continuing function within the United States Employment Service in their study of the General Aptitude Test Battery (U. S. Department of Labor, 1952), and within the Armed Forces in the study of their respective batteries of classification tests. The results of these verifications are not yet well embedded in our knowledge. In general, industry monopolizes its experience. Also any available information of this kind is in terms of occupations, not positions. Work needs to be continued in this area.

Estimates of the distributions of intelligence to be found in various civilian occupations were first reported by Fryer (1922) after World War I and later by Stewart (1957) following World War II. Both of these studies are heavily relied upon for specification of the levels of intelligence required for satisfactory performance of various occupations. They have also been the basis of various efforts to introduce level into the study of occupational choice (for example, Roe, 1956; Super, 1957).

Wilson (1952) made a systematic effort to locate similar studies of functional aptitude and achievement requirements other than intelligence. His search did not have a high yield. Since that time, studies of the antecedent circumstances differentiating between a number of kinds of later work of Harvard College sophomores has been completed by French (1959), Hagen (1960), McArthur (1954), and McArthur and Stevens (1955), and the duty assignments of airmen have been related to scores on the *Airman Classification Battery* by Tiedeman, Bryan, and Rulon (1953). Thorndike and Hagen (1959) have related those same scores to the occupational pursuits of discharged airmen. The future employment of high school students has been related to scores on aptitude tests by Bennett, Seashore, and Wesman (1952) and by Hall (1954). Also, a number of studies of the differentiating characteristics of course choices in high school (Cass and Tiedeman, 1960; Kugris and Tiedeman, 1959; Tiedeman and Sternberg, 1952) and college (Cole, 1958; Dunn, 1959; French, 1956; King, 1958; Tatsuoka, 1957; Tiedeman and Bryan, 1954; Walston, 1954; and Wilson, 1959) have been completed. Tiedeman and O'Hara (1957) concluded, after consideration of these studies, that aptitude is not a particularly strong governing force in either course or position choice. Minimum functional course or position prerequisites may be: (1) so low as to be virtually unnecessary within the restricted groups investigated;

(2) undifferentiated for the groups studied (experts don't think so in the case of high school course choices, Kugris, 1956); (3) applied in different ways by different advisers (supported in the case of high school course choices, Kugris, 1956); or (4) ignored in many instances (supported in the case of high school course choices, Kugris, 1956). Our experience has been such as to cause us to question Caplow's strong reliance upon the concept of rationalization in his description of evolutionary changes in our society over the last 150 years (Caplow, 1954). Certainly positions have become more differentiated over this period as the complexity of the economy has increased but the rational assignment of people to these positions remains an ideal far from realization. Here is another area for more research.

Education. A third subclass of functional prerequisites for positions are educational prerequisites. Entry into certain professions such as law and medicine requires pursuit of fairly well-established educational routes which include certain prescribed studies in high school, college, and graduate school. For instance, the profession of psychology is presently following the pattern of professionalization described by Caplow (1954, pp. 100-121) and ultimately may monopolize the positions of psychologist for those who have completed a prescribed pattern of courses in high school, college, and graduate school. Teaching has progressed in its professionalization to the prescription of college courses and is starting to prescribe graduate courses. Areas of religion, business, public health, public administration, architecture, engineering in its many varieties, science, and the arts are in various stages of professionalization. A variety of patterns of prerequisites exists in any of these fields, of course. There is, however, a greater homogeneity of prerequisites within any one field than there are among fields. Consequently, the course pattern a person develops as he is educated is exerting increasingly important influence on his eligibility for professional types of positions. Hence we must learn how to attend to course choices as we seek to predict position choice.

We prefer to attend to this problem by including in our grid of position choices, rows for course choices. There should be a row for each of the courses that may be pursued in junior high school, high school, junior college, trade and technical school, college, graduate school, correspondence schools, schools for extension work including study via television, schools for government service (including service in the Armed Forces) and in-service training in industry. Since no choice of courses is permitted in elementary school, provision need not be made on our grid for courses at that level. Including course choices in the grid of position choices will permit classification of position and courses in interaction. We should accomplish a more functional classification of courses and positions if we encompass the potentially vacillating flow of people from courses to positions in our consideration of the problem. A functional classification achieved in this manner will probably increase the frequency of successful predictions of position choice and continuation.

Little work has been done on the prediction of specific patterns of course choices per se. Wilson's paper (1952) and the general discussions of Cass (1956) and Kugris (1956) describe what has been done on the prediction of a curriculum available in high school. The Wilson paper and the general discussions of Dunn (1955), French (1956), and Walston (1959), report studies of the prediction of fields of concentration presented for graduation from college. A variety of course patterns can exist within both a high school curriculum and a college field of concentration, of course. Cole (1958), Congdon (1960), and Wilson (1959), recently made studies of continuation toward goal once elected. These types of study should be pursued further.

Berdie (1954) presents research concerned with some of the more immediate influences on high school students that determine choice of, and career in, college. Wolfle (1954) surveys the field of specialized talent, outlines its needs, and indicates its potential resources for the future. These works are excellent integrations of previously diverse subjects. Nevertheless, they highlight the absence of study of the flow of course and position choices. This is an area of investigation of crucial concern for the theory of career development.

Apprenticeship. A fourth subclass of positional prerequisites is the apprenticeship. A number of the trades induct members into full participation only through the apprenticeship. Educational and technical schools that are well-managed are integrated with apprentice programs of the local trades. When this happens, induction is shared by school and union and the time for induction is minimized for the participant. This is not a necessary condition of management of every vocational and technical school, however, and should be examined with care in the course and position decisions of the youth of the nation. As Caplow indicates (1954, pp. 103-111), union monopolization of positions and professionalization are one and the same thing and should constantly be scrutinized in order to insure that prerequisites are functional rather than nonfunctional.

Experience. A fifth subclass of positional prerequisites is experience. Many positions are open to the inexperienced. These are characterized as entry occupations in the *Dictionary of Occupational Titles* (U. S. Department of Labor, Division of Employment Security, 1955). Other positions have either experience or seniority requirements, for example, to superintend schools you ought to have taught. Super recently introduced the concept of occupational life spans (1957, pp. 52-68) as a means of simultaneously classifying occupations according to age of entry and age of retirement. This concept is directly applicable to the study of positions and seems worthy of considerable attention as a means of systematizing positions in a way reckoned to improve the prediction of position choice.

Experience and seniority prerequisites become outmoded as do aptitude, educational, or apprenticeship requirements. As technology and supply and demand change we should constantly review experience and seniority requirements to keep them functional.

Legal specifications. A sixth of what ought to be functional prerequisites for entry into a position are the legal prerequisites for employment. These prerequisites include such requirements as the attainment of a legal age for employment. Certain laws requiring a license to practice (for example, medicine, plumbing, teaching) or sell (for example, the liquor license) are of this kind also. These laws are presumably for the protection of the public but they effectively monopolize positions for a segment of the populace. To the degree that the holders of these special privileges exercise restraint and to the degree that the laws are consistent with current circumstances, they are functional. They may become nonfunctional or abused overnight, however, and the public needs to stand guard to change its laws in this event. Other laws permit work only in certain environmental circumstances. Many of these laws have eliminated dangers to life attendant upon the performance of particular work. Other laws, however, have effectively excluded women from certain positions. As Caplow (1954) points out, we are prone to protect the weaker sex and so, for instance, have laws limiting the number of hours women may be worked consecutively, and requiring provision of adequate rest rooms. These laws mean that women cannot legally work in some positions. Whether such laws are functional or not is hard to say. They do exist; they do limit opportunity for women; they are worthy of reconsideration now and again.

The prediction of position choice

Vocational decisions have not yet been studied very comprehensively. Yet occupational choice has been considered in relation to a number of means by which individuals may be characterized. We have considered many of these studies and, notwithstanding our realization that a general ranking eventually needs differentiation, tentatively suggest that systems of data are of the following importance to the prediction of occupational choice:

Importance	System of data
1.	The circumstances of rearing as a child including the socioeconomic status and business contacts of the family. (Friend and Haggard, 1948; Hollingshead, 1949; Jensen and Kirchner, 1955; Kahl, 1953; Lovett, 1955; McArthur, 1954; Roe, 1956; Shea, 1960; Super, 1957; Whiting, 1960.)
2.5.	A person's inventoried interests provided his orientation to careers is an "ambitious" one. (Bryan, 1960; Cass and Tiedeman, 1960; McArthur, 1954; McArthur and Stevens, 1955; Mierzwa, 1961; O'Hara and Tiedeman, 1959; Roe, 1956; Strong, 1955; Super, 1949, 1957; Tiedeman and Bryan, 1954.)
2.5.	A person's preference stated while in school provided his orientation to careers is a "responsive" one. (McArthur, 1954; McArthur and Stevens, 1955.)

Importance	System of data
4.	Values related to work and to ways of living. (Lee, 1961; Mierzwa, 1961; O'Hara and Tiedeman, 1959; Rosenberg, 1952.)
5.	Self concepts related to educational achievements and career choice.
6.	Need themes inferred from projective tests and from a person's career pattern as it exists at the time of prediction. (Berg, 1954; French, 1959; Murray, 1938; Super, 1953, 1954, 1957.)
7.	A person's career pattern (education and experience) as it exists at the time of prediction without reference to need themes (provided a record is accumulated). (Mulvey, 1961; Super, 1957.)
8.	A person's scores on achievement tests and school grades. (Wilson, 1952; Mierzwa, 1961.)
9.	Sex. (Cass and Tiedeman, 1960; Dunn, 1959; Kugris and Tiedeman, 1959.)
10.	Age. (Cass and Tiedeman, 1960; Mulvey, 1956-7.)
11.	A person's physical or mental capability. (French, 1956; Super, 1957.)
12.	A person's aptitudes. (Bennett, Seashore, and Wesman, 1952; Cass and Tiedeman, 1960; Dunn, 1959; French, 1959; Fryer, 1922; Hall, 1954; Kugris, 1956; Stewart, 1957; Super, 1949, 1957; Thorndike and Hagen, 1959; Tiedeman,

Bryan, and Rulon, 1953; Tiedeman and Sternberg, 1952.)

13.   A person's established pattern of peer relationships (for example, best friends chosen) (Herriott, 1961; Shea, 1960; Super, 1957). (The importance of this area may vary with the importance of the decision to a person. In secondary school and in later life it may rank higher in importance than indicated because of the lesser influence of decisions than in the career line. During the trial period of employment it probably has the importance designated here.)

The above ranking has the empirical support we have noted although the studies have not in general provided the needed contrasts. Since the idea of the ranking was originally formulated, Mierzwa (1961) has completed a study designed to test the order in relation to both the choice of science in high school and the perseveration of that choice during the transition from high school to college. Mierzwa studied five systems of data ascertained in grade 11 of school: ability, environment, interest, personality, and temperament. Each system was related to the presence or absence of the pursuit of a career in science as that pursuit could be ascertained both in grade 11 and one year after high school graduation (that is, the so-called thirteenth grade). The five systems of data

generally ranked in discriminatory power as follows: (1) interest; (2.5) ability and environment; (4) temperament; and (5) personality.

Mierzwa's study and other accumulating data caused us to re-formulate our original ranking, particularly to raise the import of interest in the case of ambitious careers. The above ranking is still not in complete accord with Mierzwa's data but it must be remembered that his data refers to the singular circumstance of choice of science. More data in more varied contexts are needed in order to stabilize this aspect of the problem of predicting position choices. Subsequent studies might well follow Mierzwa's lead by also focusing upon: (1) formalizing the rules of combination of data and establishing success rates for prediction systems of data already known to be related to position choice; (2) investigating presently designated systems of data in interaction with each other; and (3) introducing new systems of data into our consideration.

Only six of the systems of data known to be related to position choice are subject to control: stated preference, career pattern, school achievement, inventoried interests, self concepts, and friends. Need themes, upbringing and family status, sex, age, physical or mental disability, and aptitudes are less subject to control. If we are to understand position choice, we must incorporate into our system of prediction more of the concepts that we may control by child rearing, teaching, and counseling. Promising avenues of approach of this nature are the notions of role playing, satisfactions from role playing, and vocational maturity as presented by Super and Overstreet (1957, pp. 69-162, 1960). Herriott (1961) and Pandit also indicated that the definition subjects gave to their socioeconomic position and life chances greatly influenced their intentions toward both college and level of job. (Tiedeman and Pandit, 1958.)

Except for the extensive work of Strong (1955), the prediction of continuation of choice is less well studied than the prediction of position choice which is itself an almost virgin field as indicated above. Kibrick and Tiedeman (1960) made a reasonably extensive investigation of the continuation of the desire to become a nurse over the first six months of study in a hospital school of nursing. Perseveration of interest in nursing was largely related to the amount of consistency originally existing between a student's and her superior's conceptions of the nurse and of her role. Many relationships were significant but no outstanding effect appeared consistently among the data for the seven schools of nursing in the investigation. Walston (1959) obliquely contributed to this area in his discovery of the interdependence of self image, framed autobiographically as a college freshman, and concentration in college two years afterwards.

Congdon (1960) demonstrated that college students tend to persevere in the field of technology when there are indications of task involvement, nondefensive identification with parents, and psychological freedom in interpersonal contacts with peers. Mierzwa (1961) also dealt with perseveration upon the "path of science" as is noted above. Mierzwa's study is but a small part of a more comprehensive study of the development of scientists which Cooley (1958) has under way. Cooley's study is of the perseveration of interest in science in each of five groups of subjects who will portray the outline of development in what will eventually be overlapping units of five years each. Lee (1961) recently showed that, between college students electing science careers and those electing science teaching careers, 39 per cent of the variance is due to personality factors—interests, values, temperament. Cole (1958) and Wilson (1959) tried to ascertain whether multivariate distributions of scores on educationally relevant tests become more homogeneous as time passes and, presumably, as a college student's choices are better evaluated and more fixed. Unfortunately, in similar but not identical college contexts, the multivariate test score distributions so analyzed, both did and did not become more homogeneous. Hence, this problem needs more study.

Tatsuoka (1957) derived and evaluated a joint index of choice and of success in a group. This index is of considerable value when it is appropriate to perform one's duties in terms of an arbitrary but necessarily fixed level of success within a group.

We advance our view of the paucity of study on the fate of goal once pursued, despite existence of numerous studies of adjustment. Unfortunately, these studies of adjustment are not focused upon the criterion of perseveration itself. Most importantly, a large proportion of these studies combine positions and, frequently, even occupations. Since it may well be that satisfaction and its presumed concomitant, perseveration, are parabolic functions of the data of the predictive systems investigated in this connection (for example, Cole, Wilson, and Tiedeman, 1962), some of the often disappointing results obtained in the prediction of satisfaction may be artifacts either of the statistical procedure employed (product moment correlation which presumes linear relationships) or of the pooling of positions that should not be pooled. Since perseveration presumes choice, we feel that little is gained by studying perseveration in groups that are other than homogeneous with regard to job at the inception of the study.

Since perseveration of choice is a matter of satisfaction both with a position and with the supporting positions which define the style of life and type of identity, a position enables one to lead, we feel that systems of data for the prediction of perseveration of choice should include analyses of the role record of a person with regard to the roles associated with the attainment of identity in family (before and after marriage), in community (local, state, national, and international), and in the area of ideology (religion, politics, philosophy). The career record of a person prior to the time of prediction, analyzed both alone and in relation to the person's structure of needs is, of course, relevant here also, as Congdon (1960) shows. In the area of prediction of perseveration of choice, however, we cannot now specify systems of data of predictive efficiency in any useful way.

Self, identity, and career

Ginzberg, Ginsburg, Axelrad, and Herma (1951) and Super (1953) have proposed theories of occupational choice. Super has since greatly expanded his theory (for example, 1957) and it is now giving rise to empiric investigations (for example, Super and Overstreet, 1960). In addition, O'Hara (1957) has an unpublished paper utilizing Rogers' (1957) theory of personality both to integrate known data about career development and to develop new hypotheses in the area. Another paper by O'Hara (1959) considers talk about self in relation to Ginzberg's theory of occupational choice. This small exploration of the way youth of various ages address themselves to a statement of self in the world suggested several variants on Ginzberg's themes and particularly differences in his so-called fantasy period.

Progressive clarification, through four grade levels, of vocationally relevant self concepts was reported recently by O'Hara and Tiedeman (1959). In another study, O'Hara (1961) has a result suggesting that academic achievement in a highly selective independent school for boys is related to the degree of correspondence of the boy's estimates of his abilities, interests, and values with the estimates provided by tests. Friend and Matthews (1960) are now seeking support for further exploration of ego-identity and career through analysis of retrospective reports from groups of subjects cascaded according to age, the design of the original Ginzberg study. Walston's (1959) study clearly demonstrated the independence of a choice of curriculum in college upon the personal style one may detect in the autobiographies the students write upon arrival. Mulvey (1961) showed that the career patterns of women at midlife depend upon several elements of the high school situation of girls. Unfortunately, Wylie (1961) did not attend to the matter of vocational manifestations of self in her recent and comprehensive review of empiric studies of the self concept. Hence her study offers little but methodological guide to our problem.

Our exploration of a psychosocial theory of career

Education. Ginzberg and his associates (1951) stressed the developmental nature of their findings. Our position, while not denying Ginzberg's approach, is that, among the social forces, the school system is of primary importance in the ordering of the stages. This statement was first made in a review (Tiedeman, 1952) of the work of Ginzberg and his associates (1951). The recent work of Gribbons (1959) and Katz (1960) tends to support our position. Arguing logically it would also seem that the picture of the development of vocational self concepts as recently presented by O'Hara and Tiedeman (1959) could be changed if one were to introduce specific guidance procedures. We are inclined to think that career development is not isomorphically related to general developmental psychology. Our concern for the influence of guidance procedures within the educational setting has led us to conclude: (1) that the stages can be ordered by guidance methods, (2) that pre-eminences can be flattened or made to rise earlier to some extent, and (3) that trends can be given new direction or even reversed. These propositions need further testing.

At present we continue to study academic influences on vocational choice. It would appear that here is our best hope of solving manpower shortages in teaching, the Armed Forces, science, or other fields as needed. Previously mentioned studies of Cass (1959), Dunn (1959), and Kugris (Kugris and Tiedeman, 1959) are also of relevance to this view. In addition, Coffee (1958) has a study of the dependence of occupational realism upon social and other factors among high school boys. Pandit (Tiedeman and Pandit, 1958) has a demonstration that the level of occupation to which high school boys aspire is associated with the degree of consistency they impute to themselves and to the minds of significant others with whom they must be in relation. Herriott (1961) investigated the dependence of intended educational attainment of junior high school pupils upon the information and support the pupils have in relation to their intentions.

Shea (1960), who worked closely with the late Professor Stouffer, intends to expand knowledge of the sociopsychological circumstances of aspiration for college education. Shea is interested in the dependence of planned college attendance on social class when aptitude is held constant. He is studying this association in relation both to various types of guidance and curriculum opportunities available to sixth, seventh, eighth, and ninth-grade boys and to parental attitudes about continuation of a youth's education beyond high school. Lovett (1955) already has assembled a few data suggesting that graduation from high school when the cards are stacked against one, depends upon the attitudes of the family about education. Kahl (1953) in work with Stouffer also teased a similar finding from the data of the Harvard Mobility Study.

The interest in the career as a psychosocial phenomenon has not been singularly concentrated upon the career as it appears in youth of high school age. We have dealt with the problem over both more extended and later periods of life.

Family. Our one effort to link career and family atmosphere directly has not borne fruit. Hagen (1960), Grigg (1959), and Utton (1960) failed to verify Roe's (1957) original theory about this linkage. Roe is now engaged in efforts to refine her theory as noted earlier and has some results which verify her propositions to some extent. On the other hand, Hagen's result has refocused our own attention upon the childhood experiences. Hagen found faint dependencies of the careers of Harvard College graduates upon their family origins and the acceptance of their parents' control. He and McArthur are presently collaboratively pursuing this interest which is of long concern to McArthur. Ramsey (1959), who was also assisted by McArthur, teased out several interesting dependencies of a complex of aptitude and academic performance in college and law school upon several prior conditions of a social and cultural nature. In addition, Congdon (1960) found, as suggested by Super's (1957) theory, that continuation upon a plan to become an engineer after pursuit of a course in physics reputed to separate the sheep from the goats depends upon parental expectation, task involvement, and freedom in interpersonal relationships.

We hope that our concern with the social and personal fashioning of a career will be further illuminated by data from a study of the development of educational careers which is under the direction of Hummel (1961). This study is aimed at assessing and contrasting the commitment to career occurring within the teaching and guidance programs at Harvard. The study has excellent pre-test and post-test data, weekly diaries of students as they struggled fiercely for identification with a new group's inner coherence, and considerable but informal data on the input of faculty in and out of class. The analyses, which are formidable, were made possible by a grant from the Warren Benevolent Trust for the 1960-61 academic year. These accounts of the new professional's struggle for commitment as he leaves the liberal arts college will be quite helpful in portraying the continuing process of identification.

Reciprocity. Erikson's (1959) theory of ego-identity suggests that desired identifications must be accepted by the group or groups. Reciprocity is needed if one is to identify with a group's inner coherence. As previously noted, Pandit discovered that high school boys of high occupational aspirations have a greater consistency in concepts imputed to significant others than do boys of low aspiration. Also, Herriott has documented the heavy dependence of intended educational attainment of high school boys upon the information and support the pupils have in relation to their intentions.

The lines of interaction of career and society are being further explored by Massimo who is assisted by a grant through the Judge Baker Guidance Center from the National Institute of Mental Health. Essentially, Massimo plans to investigate the widening of freedom for psychotherapy and remedial tutoring which might become available to aggressive, adolescent delinquents in a somewhat sheltered job. After Massimo helps a predelinquent to find a job, he plans to act as supervisor-tutor-therapist for the boy. It is hoped that work may become the keystone in the arch of the ego strength needed for further rehabilitation.

Our concern for the psychosocial aspects of career includes an interest not only in the interactions of person with family, school, and job situation but also in the sex role. The studies of Cass (1959), Dunn (1959), and Kugris (1959) early noted the considerable dependence of educational pursuits upon sex. The census further attests that men and women pursue different endeavors. Several years ago we decided that a separate theory of career development was needed for men and women. Studies by Tyler (1951) and O'Hara (1962) revealed differential career patterns very early in life. We decided to concentrate on a theory for men. Several students had different ideas. Matthews (1960) has completed a rather extensive investigation of women's attitudes about marriage and career in relation to their age, educational inclinations, and life plan about marriage and career. Deutsch's (1944) theory on feminity and creativity early attracted and held Matthews' interest. Although controversial, the Deutsch theory is still one of the intriguing aspects of the several formal propositions about career development in women that Matthews has developed and eventually hopes to be able to test in several ways. Mulvey (1961) related a modified version of Super's (1957) career patterns for mature women both to their educational and social circumstances while in high school and to their satisfaction with life and intentions about modifying that life. As a result of these several investigations we are coming to think that the kind of resolution a woman achieves of her sex role is of major influence in her career. This relationship needs further clarification.

Bibliography

Allport, Gordon, Vernon, P. E., and Lindzey, G. *Study of Values*, Manual, third edition (Boston: Houghton Mifflin Company, 1960).

Bennett, George K., Seashore, Harold G., and Wesman, Alexander G. "Aptitude Testing: Does it 'Prove Out' in Counseling Practice?" 30 *Occupations* (May 1952), 584-598.

Berdie, Ralph F. *After High School — What?* (Minneapolis: University of Minnesota Press, 1954).

Berg, Irwin. "Comment on Career Patterns as a Basis for Vocational Counseling," 1 *Journal of Counseling Psychology* (1954), 19-20.

Bidwell, C. E., and McArthur, C. C. "Values, Careers and Higher Education: A Comparison of Two Generations of Harvard Undergraduates," mimeo (Cambridge: the authors, Harvard University, 1960).

Blau, Peter M., Gustad, J. W., Jessor, R., Parnes, H. S., and Wilcock, R. C. "Occupational Choice: A Conceptual Framework," 9 *Industrial Labor Relations Review* (1956), 531-543.

Blocher, D. H., and Schutz, R. A. "Relationships Among Self-Descriptions, Occupational Stereotypes, and Vocational Preferences," 8 *Journal of Counseling Psychology* (1961), 314-317.

Bordin, Edward S., and Wilson, Earl H. "Change of Interest as a Function of Shift in Curricular Orientation," 13 *Educational and Psychological Measurement* (1953), 297-307.

Brophy, A. L. "Self, Role, and Satisfaction," 59 *Genetic Psychological Monographs* (1959), 263-308.

Bryan, Joseph G. *A Method for the Exact Determination of the Characteristic Equation and Latent Vectors of a Matrix with Applications to the Discriminant Function for More Than Two Groups* (Cambridge: unpublished doctoral dissertation, Harvard Graduate School of Education, 1950).

Buchheimer, Arnold, and Balogh, S. C. *The Counseling Relationship* (Chicago: Science Research Associates, 1961).

Caplow, Theodore. *The Sociology of Work* (Minneapolis: University of Minnesota Press, 1954).

Cass, John C. *Prediction of Curriculum Choice in Maine Secondary Schools* (Cambridge: unpublished doctoral dissertation, Harvard Graduate School of Education, 1956).

Cass, John C., and Tiedeman, David V. "Vocational Development and the Election of a High School Curriculum," 38 *Personnel and Guidance Journal* (1960), 538-545.

Coffee, James M. *Occupational Realism: An Analysis of Factors Influencing Realism in the Occupational Planning of Male High School Seniors* (Cambridge: unpublished doctoral dissertation, Harvard Graduate School of Education, 1957).

Cole, Joseph W. *The Effect of Migration on the Multivariate Test Score Distribution Patterns for College Students Classified According to Curriculum Groups* (Cambridge: unpublished doctoral dissertation, Harvard Graduate School of Education, 1958).

Cole, Joseph W., Wilson, Kenneth M., and Tiedeman, David V. *Dispersion Analysis and the Search for Educational Goals in College: A Study in Duplicate*, mimeo (Cambridge: the junior author, 17 Sumner Road, January 1962).

Congdon, Robert. *Orientation to Parents, Capacity for Task Involvement, and Patterns of Interpersonal Relationships as Sources of Variation in the Responses of Male College Students to the Vocational Selection of a Technology Curriculum* (Cambridge: unpublished doctoral dissertation, Harvard Graduate School of Education, 1960).

Cooley, William W. "Attributes of Potential Scientists," 28 *Harvard Educational Review* (winter 1958), 1-18.

Deutsch, Helene. *The Psychology of Women: A Psychoanalytic Interpretation, Vol. I and II* (New York: Grune & Stratton, Inc., 1944).

Dorcus, Roy M., and Jones, Margaret Hubbard. *Handbook of Employee Selection* (New York: McGraw-Hill Book Co., Inc., 1950).

Dunn, Frances E. *Guiding College Students in the Selection of a Field of Concentration* (Cambridge: unpublished doctoral dissertation, Harvard Graduate School of Education, 1955).

————. "Two Methods of Predicting the Selection of a College Major," 6 *Journal of Counseling Psychology* (1959), 15-26.

Englander, M. "A Psychological Analysis of Vocational Choice: Teaching," 7 *Journal of Counseling Psychology* (1960), 257-264.

Erikson, Erik H. *Childhood and Society* (New York: W. W. Norton, Inc., 1950).

————. "Identity and the Life Cycle," 1 *Psychological Issues* (1959), 1-171.

Forrest, Aubrey L. "Persistence of Vocational Choice of the Merit Scholarship Winners," 39 *Personnel and Guidance Journal* (1961), 466-471.

French, Wendell L. *The Relationship Between Various Measures Recorded on a Selected Group of Harvard Undergraduates and Occupation Twelve Years Later* (Cambridge: unpublished doctoral dissertation, Harvard Graduate School of Education, 1956).

————. "Can a Man's Occupation be Predicted?" 6 *Journal of Counseling Psychology* (1959), 95-99.

Friend, Jeannette G., and Haggard, Ernest A. "Work Adjustment in Relation to Family Background," 16 *Applied Psychology Monographs* (1948).

Friend, Jeannette G., and Matthews, Esther. "Aspects of Identity Formation in the Career Development of Girls and Women: A Pilot Project," mimeo (Newton, Mass.: the junior author, Newton South High School, 1960).

Fryer, D. "Occupational Intelligence Standards," 16 *School and Society* (1922), 273-277.

Ginzberg, Eli, Ginsburg, Sol W., Axelrad, Sidney, and Herma, John L. *Occupational Choice: An Approach to a General Theory* (New York: Columbia University Press, 1951).

Gribbons, Warren D. *Determination of Progress in Educational and Vocational Planning in Adolescence* (Cambridge: unpublished doctoral dissertation, Harvard

Graduate School of Education, 1959).

Grigg, A. E. "Childhood Experience with Parental Attitudes: A Test of Roe's Hypothesis," 6 *Journal of Counseling Psychology* (1959), 153-156.

Grunes, Willa F. "On Perception of Occupations," 34 *Personnel and Guidance Journal* (1956), 276-279.

Hagen, Douglas. "Careers and Family Atmospheres: An Empirical Test of Roe's Theory," 7 *Journal of Counseling Psychology* (1960), 251-256.

Hall, C. S., and Lindzey, G. *Theories of Personality* (New York: John Wiley and Sons, Inc., 1957).

Hall, Robert C. *A Study of the Relationship Among Certain Occupational Groups in Performance on the Differential Aptitude Test Battery* (Storrs, Conn.: unpublished doctoral dissertation, University of Connecticut, 1954).

Havighurst, Robert J. *Human Development and Education* (New York: Longmans, Green and Co., 1953).

Hemphill, John R. "Administration as Problem Solving," in Halpin, Andrew W. (ed.), *Administrative Theory in Education* (Chicago: Midwest Administration Center, University of Chicago, 1958), 89-118.

Herriott, Robert. *Some Social Determinants of Level of Educational Aspirations*, mimeo (Cambridge: D. V. Tiedeman, 17 Sumner Road, August 1961).

Hilton, Thomas L. "Career Decision-Making," 9 *Journal of Counseling Psychology* (1962), 291-298.

Hollingshead, August B. *Elmtown's Youth* (New York: John Wiley and Sons, Inc., 1949).

Hoppock, Robert. "A Twenty-Seven Year Follow-up on Job Satisfaction of Employed Adults," 38 *Personnel and Guidance Journal* (1960), 489-492.

Hottel, Althea K., director. *How Fare Women? A Report of the Commission on the Education of Women of the American Council on Education* (Washington, D. C.: The American Council on Education, 1955).

Hummel, Raymond C. *Program Report on the Development of Educational Careers Study*, mimeo (Cambridge: the author, 13 Kirkland Street, April 1961).

Jensen, Paul G., and Kirchner, Wayne K. "A National Answer to the Question 'Do Sons Follow Their Fathers' Occupations?'" 39 *Journal of Applied Psychology* (1955), 419-421.

Kahl, Joseph A. "Educational and Occupational Aspirations of 'Common Man' Boys," 23 *Harvard Educational Review* (summer 1953), 186-203.

Katz, Martin. *The Development and Evaluation of a Guidance Text for Eighth or Ninth Grade* (Cambridge: unpublished doctoral dissertation, Harvard Graduate School of Education, 1960).

Kibrick, Anne, and Tiedeman, David V. "Conceptions of Self and Perception of Role in Relation to Continuation in Schools of Nursing," 8 *Journal of Counseling Psychology*, (1961), 62-69.

King, Richard G. *The Prediction of Undergraduate Field of Concentration in Harvard College* (Cambridge: published doctoral dissertation, the author, Harvard College, 1958).

Kugris, Violet. *A Study of the Allocation of Differential Aptitudes for Various High School Curricula in Terms of Pupil Choice and Counselor Opinion* (Cambridge: unpublished doctoral dissertation, Harvard Graduate School of Education, 1956).

Kugris, Violet, and Tiedeman, David V. *"You Ought to Study . . ."; Method and Results in Relation to the Election of a Curriculum in Secondary School,* mimeo (Cambridge: the junior author, 17 Sumner Road, 1959).

Leary, Timothy. *Interpersonal Diagnosis of Personality* (New York: The Ronald Press, 1957).

Lee, Eugene C. *Career Development of Science Teachers: Personality Determinants at the Exploratory Stage* (Cambridge: unpublished doctoral dissertation, Harvard Graduate School of Education, 1961).

Levine, Carol. *Taped interviews on the vocational situation defined by children in elementary school* (Cambridge: D. V. Tiedeman, 17 Sumner Road, 1959).

Lovett, Stephen K. *The Post-Secondary School Adjustment of Matched Groups of Graduates and Drop-outs with Special Reference to Underlying Familial Differences* (Cambridge: unpublished doctoral dissertation, Harvard Graduate School of Education, 1955).

Maslow, Abraham. *Motivation and Personality* (New York: Harper and Bros., 1954).

Matthews, Esther. *The Marriage-Career Conflict in the Career Development of Girls and Young Women* (Cambridge: unpublished doctoral dissertation, Harvard Graduate School of Education, 1960).

McArthur, Charles C. "Long Term Validity of the Strong Interest Test in Two Subcultures," 38 *Journal of Applied Psychology* (1954), 346-353.

McArthur, Charles C., and Stevens, Lucia Beth. "The Validation of Expressed Interests as Compared with Inventoried Interests: A Fourteen-Year Follow-up," 39 *Journal of Applied Psychology* (1955), 184-198.

Mierzwa, John A. *The Differentiation of Career Choice: A Study of the Choice of a Career in Science During a Two-Year Period in Late Adolescence* (Cambridge: unpublished doctoral dissertation, Harvard Graduate School of Education, 1961).

Miller, Delbert C., and Form, William H. *Industrial Sociology* (New York: Harper and Bros., 1951).

Mulvey, Mary C. *Research on the Older Worker and Its Implications for Career Development—with Supplement* (Cambridge: unpublished special paper, Harvard Graduate School of Education, 1956, 1957).

————. *Psychological and Sociological Factors in the Prediction of Career Patterns of Women* (Cambridge: unpublished doctoral dissertation, Harvard Graduate School of Education, 1961).

Murray, Henry A. *Explorations in Personality* (New York: Oxford University Press, 1938).

Newman, Joel. *Taped interviews on value positions of young adolescent boys* (Cambridge: D. V. Tiedeman, 17 Sumner Road, 1959).

O'Hara, Robert P. *On the Importance of the Self Concept to a General Theory of Occupational Choice* (Cambridge: unpublished special paper, Harvard Graduate School of Education, 1957).

_____. *Talk About Self: The Results of a Pilot Series of Interviews in Relation to Ginzberg's Theory of Occupational Choice,* mimeo (Cambridge: D. V. Tiedeman, 17 Sumner Road, 1959).

_____. *The Relationship of Vocational Self Concept to Achievement in High School,* typewritten (Chestnut Hill, Mass.: the author, Boston College, 1961).

_____. "The Roots of Careers," 62 *Elementary School Journal* (1962), 277-280.

_____. *Vocational Self-Concepts: Boys Choosing Science and Non-Science Careers,* typewritten (New York: College Entrance Examination Board, 1963).

O'Hara, Robert P., and Tiedeman, David V. "Vocational Self Concepts in Adolescence," 6 *Journal of Counseling Psychology* (1959), 292-301.

Paterson, Donald G., Gerken, C. d'A., and Hahn, Milton E. *Revised Minnesota Occupational Rating Scales* (Minneapolis: University of Minnesota Press, 1953).

Ramsey, Robert R., Jr. *A Study of Cultural Influence on Academic Performance in College and Law School* (Cambridge: unpublished doctoral dissertation, Harvard Graduate School of Education, 1959).

Roe, Anne. *The Psychology of Occupations* (New York: John Wiley and Sons, Inc., 1956).

_____. "Early Determinants of Vocational Choices," 4 *Journal of Counseling Psychology* (1957), 212-217.

_____. *Origin of Interests,* mimeo (Cambridge: the author, 17 Sumner Road, 1961).

Rogers, Carl. *Client-Centered Therapy* (Boston: Houghton Mifflin Company, 1951).

Rosenberg, Morris. *Occupations and Values* (New York: Free Press of Glencoe, 1957).

Shea, Paul D. *A Critical Review of the Research Literature on Social Factors Relating to Educational Mobility* (Cambridge: unpublished special paper, Harvard Graduate School of Education, 1960).

Smith, M. B., Bruner, J. S., and White, R. W. *Opinions and Personality* (New York: John Wiley and Sons, Inc., 1956).

Stewart, Naomi. "AGCT Scores of Army Personnel Grouped by Occupations," 26 *Occupations* (1957), 5-41.

Strong, Edward K., Jr. *Vocational Interests 18 Years After College* (Minneapolis: University of Minnesota Press, 1955).

Sullivan, Harry Stack. *The Interpersonal Theory of Psychiatry* (New York: Harper and Bros., 1953).

Super, Donald E. *Appraising Vocational Fitness by Means of Psychological Tests* (New York: Harper and Bros., 1949).

_____. "A Theory of Vocational Development," 8 *American Psychologist* (1953), 185-190.

_____. "Career Patterns as a Basis for Vocational Counseling," 1 *Journal of Counseling Psychology* (1954), 12-20.

_____. *The Psychology of Careers* (New York: Harper and Bros., 1957).

Super, Donald E., and Bachrach, Paul B. *Scientific Careers and Vocational Development Theory* (New York: Bureau of Publications, Teachers College, Columbia University, 1957).

Super, Donald E., Crites, J. O., Hummel, R. C., Moser, Helen P., Overstreet, Phoebe L., and Warnath, C. F. *Vocational Development: A Framework for Research* (New York: Bureau of Publications, Teachers College, Columbia University, 1957).

Super, Donald E., and Overstreet, Phoebe L. *The Vocational Maturity of Ninth-Grade Boys* (New York Bureau of Publications, Teachers College, Columbia University, 1960).

Tageson, C. F. *The Relationship of Self Perceptions to Realism of Vocational Preference* (Washington, D.C.: Catholic University of America Press, 1960).

Tatsouka, Maurice M. *Joint Probability of Membership and Success in a Group: An Index Which Combines the Information from Discriminant and Regression Analyses as Applied to the Guidance Problem* (Cambridge: unpublished doctoral dissertation, Harvard Graduate School of Education, 1957).

Thorndike, Robert L., and Hagen, Elizabeth. *10,000 Careers* (New York: John Wiley and Sons, Inc., 1959).

Tiedeman, David V. "Occupational Choice: An Approach to a General Theory: A Review," 22 *Harvard Educational Review* (1952), 184-190.

————. "Decision and Vocational Development: A Paradigm and Its Implications," 40 *Personnel and Guidance Journal* (1961), 15-20.

Tiedeman, David V., and Bryan, Joseph G. "Prediction of College Field of Concentration," 24 *Harvard Educational Review* (1954), 122-139.

Tiedeman, David V., Bryan, Joseph G., and Rulon, Phillip J. *The Utility of the Airman Classification Battery for Assignment of Airmen to Eight Air Force Specialties*, second printing (Cambridge: Educational Research Corporation, 10 Craigie Street, 1953).

Tiedeman, David V., and O'Hara, Robert P. "Preparedness and the Freedom To Choose One's Occupation," in Gruber, Frederick C. (ed.), *The Good Education of Youth* (Philadelphia: University of Pennsylvania Press, 1957), 229-248.

Tiedeman, David V., and Pandit, Jiwan Lal. *On Identity and Level of Occupational Aspiration*, mimeo (Cambridge: the senior author, 17 Sumner Road, 1958).

Tiedeman, David V., and Sternberg, Jack J. "Information Appropriate for Curriculum Guidance," 22 *Harvard Educational Review* (1952), 257-274

Tyler, Leona. "The Relationship of Interests to Abilities and Reputations Among First Grade Children," 11 *Educational and Psychological Measurement* (1951), 255-264.

————. "Toward a Workable Psychology of Individuality," 14 *American Psychology* (1959), 75-81.

————. "Research Explorations in the Realm of Choice," 8 *Journal of Counseling Psychology* (1961), 195-201.

U. S. Department of Labor, U. S. Employment Service, Bureau of Employment Security. *Guide to the Use of*

General Aptitude Test Battery, B-1002: I. Administration; II. Scoring Directions and Norms; III. Development (Washington, D.C.: The Department of Labor, July 1952).

U. S. Department of Labor, Division of Employment Security. *Dictionary of Occupational Titles*, second edition, supplement no. 1 (Washington, D.C.: U. S. Government Printing Office, 1955).

U. S. Department of Labor, Division of Employment Security. *Estimates of Worker Trait Requirements for 4,000 Jobs as Defined in Dictionary of Occupational Titles* (Washington, D.C.: U. S. Printing Office, 1956, correction lists, 1958).

Utton, A. *Recalled Parent-Child Relations as Determinants of Vocational Choice* (New York: unpublished doctoral dissertation, Teachers College, Columbia University, 1960).

Walston, Ernest B. *The Autobiography in the Prediction of College Field of Concentration*, typewritten (Cambridge: D. V. Tiedeman, 17 Sumner Road, 1959).

Weitz, Henry. "Guidance as Behavior Change," 39 *Personnel and Guidance Journal* (1961), 550-560.

White, Robert W. *Lives in Progress* (New York: Holt, Rinehart & Winston, Inc., 1952).

Whiting, John W. M. "Resource Mediation and Learning by Identification," in Iscol, I., and Stevenson, H. (eds.), *Personality Development in Children* (Austin: University of Texas Press, 1960).

Wilson, Kenneth M. *Correlates of Career Developments: A Review of the Literature*, mimeo (Cambridge: D. V. Tiedeman, 17 Sumner Road, 1952).

————. *The Effect of Changes in Fields of Study on the Dispersion of Antecedent Multivariate Test Distributions for College Field of Concentration Groups* (Cambridge: unpublished doctoral dissertation, Harvard Graduate School of Education, 1959).

Wolfle, Dael. *America's Resources of Specialized Talent* (New York: Harper and Bros., 1954).

Wylie, Ruth C. *The Self Concept* (Lincoln: University of Nebraska Press, 1961).

Appendix A

Career and personality:
An illustration of synthesis

by Rhoda W. Baruch

Career in personality

What adjustive functions of personality are served by the choice and pursuit of a career? This question, analogous to the one raised by Smith, Bruner, and White (1956, p. 39) with regard to opinions and personality, is based on the assumption that the total behavior of a person, including his vocational choices and vocational role enactment, reflects certain regularities of functioning. Behavior, and specifically vocational behavior, becomes predictable in terms of this underlying regularity and the description of this regularity is the description of the personality.

A career, in the Murray (1938) model of personality, is a serial, a longer functional unit of behavior which is defined as "a directionally organized intermittent succession of proceedings" (Hall and Lindzey, 1957, p. 167). It can be studied by getting records of critical proceedings along its course and noting indices of development such as changes in disposition and increase in knowledge, as well as continuity of thema. A Murray construct, important for the study of careers, is ordination, which is a higher mental process on the same level as cognition, and involves the plan-making function, and the setting up of subgoals and schedules. Such schedules reduce conflict among competing needs and goal objects by arranging for the expression of these tendencies at different times.

This ordination is apparently the same process as those called crystallization, choice, and clarification in Section IV of this paper. That paradigm of vocational development involves a sequence of organizations of fields and goals. Successive organizations of fields and goals are functionally related. The paradigm and the Murray personality model seem to complement each other. One is tempted to infer needs from goals and press from fields and to study the successive schema which the ego functions organize.

Perhaps the greatest contribution that Murray could make to career theory would be procedural. Murray and his colleagues intensively studied normal personalities with numerous sessions and procedures conducted by different examiners who worked independently until at a final session they met to exchange findings and interpretations (Murray, 1938, pp. 705-8). In this way the experimenter could discover the operating variables in a manner that is often impossible in the more statistical and rigorous procedures. Murray argued that "our plan provides the conditions that enhance the evolution of an effective policy of experimental action." And, of course, successive formulations of personality were attempted with prediction within this system made possible for the individual's behavior.

The case material described herein was obtained from the files of the intensive personality studies conducted at the Harvard Psychological Clinic. The original studies followed the pattern described by

Murray in *Explorations in Personality,* using multiple procedures and investigators and with a senior staff or Diagnostic Council member responsible for evaluating and interpreting the results. The subjects, students at the college during the period 1938-41, were paid for their participation and some of them were asked to return several years later for further study. These were studies of normal adolescence and the later follow-up project was focused on the normal growth of personality. Each case includes a vast amount of data, enough, surely, to learn something about the career in the context of the personality development. However, it should be pointed out that these case materials were not initially compiled with any special interest in careers, so that certain desirable data, such as records of part-time work, vocational interest inventories, and interviews focused on careers were not included. Though not ideal for our current study, these volumes of case materials were nonetheless very valuable as a source.

As one reads through the voluminous material comprising one case: a written autobiography, reports on the somatotype, speech analysis, intelligence tests, hypnotic experiments, thematic apperception test, thematic completion tests, thematic alternative tests, several verbatim interviews focused on particular matters with the subject, one interview with his mother, Rorschach Test, handwriting analysis, and many themes written for college English classes, one gets a feeling for the complexity of a human being and yet the sense of some unity so that one feels one can formulate a personality.

The selection of materials and organization for this formulation is a complex task. If we wish to ask the question, "What adjustive function does this career fulfill in the context of this personality?" we focus on those aspects of the case which we feel are most significant for this kind of study.

That the career emerges in a particular societal setting and at a particular time in history cannot be ignored. This generation grew up during a depression and faced a major war upon graduation, both important determinants of their career patterns. Also, as a group, this generation may have placed more emphasis on the career as a means of expressing instrumental activism than the current generation does (Bidwell and McArthur, 1960). The social and economic realities impinging on these individuals were no doubt influences on the career, although they are not the specific content of this study and must be remembered as part of the general background. Simple generalizations from specific instances about personality as related to careers are cautioned against because of changing social and economic factors and because each individual personality is likely to express itself in a career in a unique way.

To study the individual case, we might choose as a point of departure the systems of data which vocational psychologists have rated highest in importance for predicting of vocational choices (see Section V). The circumstances of rearing as a child, including the socioeconomic status and business contacts of the family, comprise one such system of data. The subject's own stated choice in school is a second important system of data along with the process of ordination, and so forth.

A third and most interesting system of data for this writer consists of the need themes inferred from all the available data and their relationship to the career. What continuities in such strivings can be discerned in the career and in other aspects of the personality? A study of the personality on several levels, as suggested by Leary (1957, pp. 75-83), is required for this kind of analysis. Knowledge of the traits, capacities, skills, and strengths are required to observe the ways in which the subject mediates between his press and his needs or organizes his fields and goals.

The Case of John Chatwell

Family background and early development. John Chatwell, in his autobiography, described his family as of the "so-called upper-middle strata," among the oldest on the continent, and of English descent. His father was a free-lance research scientist who had received his doctorate and had contributed to the support of his family while still a student. Chatwell said of his father, "Need during his youth brought home the value of struggle, and he is today largely the result of his own effort." Although his father's career was viewed as successful, it was throughout "dogged with business men who have profited greatly by his creations, and at the same time have left little for him." When Chatwell was a man of 28 he remembered that "as a boy I always had some idea of vindicating my father's injuries that he had re-

ceived at the hands of the world. . . ." He referred here to the "pitfalls and turmoils and disappointments that come the way of inventors."

Chatwell was outspoken in his admiration for his father's versatility and competence, but made frequent reference to his being intensely nervous and dogmatic, which "made for a certain amount of friction with those about him most of the time." Chatwell remembered that "I used to be so scared when my father bawled me out, that was enough. It was mainly an appeal to reason." If his father was often "distant and short-tempered," and as Chatwell recalled, "I've been madder at him than at anyone else," the father was also sympathetic inside and would occasionally indulge his son by "coming through with something that would floor you."

The subject's mother studied history and philosophy at college, biology in graduate school, and has taught school intermittently since her marriage. At the time of the second study she had been appointed dean of women at a small college. Chatwell characterized his mother and all of her sisters as "women of patience, generosity, and great humor." His mother was "extremely affectionate and sympathetic and exhibits in her work a marked degree of executive ability." Although she too was "highly nervous," she was more likely to give up her own objectives for the sake of peace. In his rearing, his mother emphasized independence, so that Chatwell dressed himself, for example, at an early age, "especially because I was the oldest."

Chatwell described his home life as interesting

and stimulating, although not peaceful. He emphasized the productivity, ("Dad is always making something, as are all his children") and the bickering, which was "continual, generally healthy, but occasionally bitter." In such arguments, Chatwell was usually aligned with his mother, and his brother and father were on the opposing side. These were never arguments of great consequence. About important issues, there was great family solidarity. In general, as an adult, Chatwell's sentiments and ethical ideas conformed to his parents', he reported.

Chatwell's siblings included one brother who was two years younger than he, another brother who was fourteen years his junior, and a sister who was five years younger than he. The brother who was closest in age to Chatwell and the latter had done many things together. "We entertained highly imaginative illusions about the vessels and vehicles that we intended to build and in which we intended to explore the smallest part of the universe." This brother was athletic, restless, antisocial, and highly imaginative. Surly and "stubborn to the point of pain," he would "fly off the handle easily" and occasionally this brother had beaten up Chatwell. Chatwell had only recently paid any attention to his sister and this was in the role of adviser and confidant, and his youngest brother, although "the most dominating influence in the house" had had little importance in Chatwell's life, he reported.

With regard to his early development, Chatwell tells us he was precocious, that he played, generally by himself, with tools, motors, and so forth, and that his attitude when young was obedient, but when older, especially at school, he was "critical, aggressive, belligerent, but often cooperative." He had at school many casual friendships and three deep ones. There were quarrels, "but not with friends."

Of the community in which he grew up, Chatwell said it was an intellectual and wealthy one, with professional people predominating. He attended local private schools with very small classes, and he especially enjoyed philosophy. He remarked, ". . . and as is only natural with men who are studying the abstract, much of the classwork was in the form of argument and debate, a trend which held sway in the other courses, too."

In the secondary school, Chatwell was president of a fraternity, a member of the student council, and a member of the football team. (His mother reported that he was usually on the periphery at a football game.) Chatwell felt that although he might experience joy after a victory in football, this experience was of a "transient variety" and greater joy could be experienced from contemplation of a perfect marriage or a perfect solution to a philosophical question.

In high school Chatwell's best subjects were English and sciences and his worst subjects were languages. His interests were in his fraternity, his radio station, football, and his girl.

At his school, Chatwell fell in love with a girl whose affection he eventually won away from his best friend. He remained interested in her through his first year in college and said, "We seriously considered marriage, but at a stage necessarily advanced because of the long period of time that would have to transpire before the completion of my education." When he later gave up this girl in favor of another one "closer to his ideal," he said of this new girl, "She typifies home and rest and a working partnership in some duty to a society that we two can perform better than anyone else." (Chatwell was at this time already in Harvard and the local branch of his church there emphasized service rather than education.)

All of this early history derives from Chatwell's autobiography, interviews which took place in both studies and questionnaire responses. Except for a few parenthetical remarks, it is the subject's view of his background written from his point of view (Leary's Level II and sometimes Level V). The themes which he has brought to the foreground here will be encountered again and again and we will observe how these presage his career development. The continuity of his story was supplied by this writer and is not Chatwell's.

A stated vocational preference and the search for an identity. When, as a sophomore in Harvard, Chatwell first enrolled as a subject in the study, he gave as his vocational choice the patent law. He had an uncle who was a member of this profession and an aunt had suggested this to him when he was fourteen or fifteen years old. He wrote of his plans as follows: "My immediate ambition is to prepare myself for the practice of patent law by the studies of sciences in college and of law in some graduate school. After

that, I wish to strike out in that field, which I consider fascinating and suitable for one of my mental equipment and temperament. It may be, however, that heredity will assert itself and divert me into the paths of pedagogy—I have felt strong urges in that direction. It may also be that I shall go into politics from the law; I don't know."

Chatwell had a serial program, but the process of ordination did not proceed completely smoothly. On the contrary, Chatwell experienced something very much like what Erikson calls, "an identity crisis."

First, the summer before Chatwell entered Harvard, he experienced despair. He had gone to a church convention and stayed at his girl's house. He took a sales job in that town and stayed on at her house, although the girl left for Europe. He did poorly at the job and told his family he did well and was living at the Y, whereas he was "sponging" at his girl's house. He was in an auto collision while driving a borrowed car and there was a law suit and hard feelings. This attempt at independence was very disappointing. In a freshman theme on growth, Chatwell wrote, "You realized, for example, the utter aloneness of the man who tries to worry things out by himself. You realized the tremendous urge that is in every man to lay his load at the feet of someone stronger and wiser than he, for at times it seemed as if there were no possible way to work out your own solution."

While at Harvard, a girl friend of his gave him up in favor of a more aggressive "continental-type" Tech man. He later became more aggressive with women, he reported.

Chatwell changed his field of concentration from the biochemical sciences to psychology. (This change may have occurred as a consequence of his participation as a subject at the clinic, an example of the act of observation distorting the observation. Chatwell was a very eager subject, dropping into the clinic office frequently to help compile the "Chatwell dossier," and acted as an eager subject in various public demonstrations of hypnosis.)

Toward the end of his sophomore year, Chatwell spoke of his problems as follows. " 'Where in the world am I,' as Cicero said. I need complete reorientation, I don't know where I stand. Should I be in college? How shall I fit myself for what I want to do? What do I want to do? I live entirely in the present and do not face the future. I want to live widely, travel, hear music, and so forth. I'm worried about money. Work does not seem to interest me much. I don't seem to have any guts and I don't seem to care."

About one year later in his junior year, he said, "I don't enjoy things as I used to. The grass on the other side always looks greener. I do things now just to get through—whether drunk or sober, falling in love or out, and so forth. I don't read books with the same enjoyment. I just read them fast to get through."

At about this time (end of junior year) Chatwell was discussing anger in an interview on emotion and control. He said he hadn't lost his temper for four or five years; the last time was in high school when he was incorrectly accused of something by the principal. However, he continued, "Last Monday I was angry over the unreasonableness of an employer. A cold, dead calm with autonomic manifestations (breathing, and so forth) and a lot of analyses. As a kid I had a terrific temper. But I take a great delight in being calm when the other fellow is mad. Ordinarily now things don't matter enough to me to get mad. I'm very subject to just plain ordinary anxiety. Waiting for people, appointments, girls sometimes, examinations, never. Gastric tightness, smoking like hell, dry mouth." (Note—rich as the case material is, there is no other reference to the employer mentioned above and we have no full record of Chatwell's part-time work experiences.)

During his senior year, Chatwell complained again about his interest declining. He couldn't work or play unless he was interested. He started new enterprises with zest, but as with girls, faults soon came out and he had to get out of the situation.

After getting behind in his work, he began to wonder if it were worth while, anyway. What if he didn't graduate? He wondered about the value of education, "Does it make anyone better or happier, does it make the world better?"

His special pleasure in school, he reported, was to argue, especially if he knew nothing about the subject. He said the trouble with Harvard was "too many textbooks." He liked to argue in class and the instructor got pretty confused, but the instructor "must win because he has a position to maintain." Chatwell and his two roommates overwhelmed a tutor at a party and whenever the tutor tried to open his mouth, one of them would cut in "bang" with an argument. Chatwell argued that "A" students at Harvard have "regurgitative" minds and he could beat them in any argument. According to the Graduate Record Examination, he said, he knew more than the concentrators in their own fields. He did not go out for debating because being taken in or rejected depended on the whim of the officers. The class elections were also run irregularly and unjustly. But what could he do? It seemed futile and he didn't see why the boys couldn't have their fun.

He no longer cared so much for girls because he wasn't afraid of them anymore and he no longer sweated driving in traffic. He occasionally found himself acting, speaking in dialect, or bowing and clicking his heels when he met someone. He had no fixed personality of his own, but readily fell in with his environment, he complained.

Toward the end of his senior year, Chatwell applied for the Marine Corps and was rejected because of his defective vision. He expected to be drafted after graduation and looked forward to Army life, saying he would try to work up as an officer. He was confident of getting a civilian job, and had had several offers already, but thought the Army would be a good temporary career. "The war will last a while," he thought.

Chatwell had a good part-time job as a senior, arranging a radio program which involved information contests between teams of high school pupils. His job was to get the teams, which involved persuading the principal, overcoming the prejudice of school boards, and selling the idea that an educational purpose was being served. "This was duck soup for me," he said.

Since his mind was off school, he was happier. He was busy during the day and had a new girl to make love to in the evening.

About Harvard, he learned it was easy to coast through, like any other place. As a freshman, he had started to try out for the dramatic club, but became disgusted with "the system" and quit. He did swimming for exercise but did not try for the team. He said this was a case of a big frog in a big puddle, for at home he had been top in everything.

As a senior, Chatwell spoke about his daydream: a farm that is self-sufficient with its own source of electricity and with difficulties to overcome independently. He hoped to retire to this farm and he included his latest girl in this dream.

Also during his senior year, Chatwell enrolled in a course in public speaking, but attended and spoke only once. He was required to make one long speech and by an oversight, he missed the date of this speech. He needed the credit to graduate, and although he tried to "bring his powers to bear on the instructor," the instructor was tough and he did not graduate as scheduled. He then "raised merry hell with the local draft board" and succeeded in getting a deferment so that he could return to summer school to complete his credit requirements.

Years later Chatwell said that two things stood out for him in his senior year, meeting the girl he finally married and "flunking public speaking." These were for him "the first important thing I ever did right and the last important thing I ever did wrong."

Upon graduation, Chatwell did not wait to be

drafted, but enlisted in the regular Army Air Corps. The most important consideration in this decision was that he thought his chances for a commission would be greater. The commission became a matter of paramount importance for, "in addition to the monetary, social, and other obvious aspects of officer status, there was the pressing motive that a commission would make it possible to marry."

After a few weeks of severe and "inferior" training, Chatwell decided that "God helps only a few of us, and he seemed to be ignoring me." He applied for and got the job of mathematics instructor and was thus relieved of the unpleasant duties and brought into "daily contact with excellent and congenial officers." He found he had no difficulty handling classes of 500 men, although he realized that military discipline made the task easier, and through this experience his opinion of himself was inflated, he wrote. An important factor was his winning the respect of the other men.

When the Army discontinued this mathematics training program, Chatwell was given a job of "considerable magnitude and responsibility." It involved scheduling the activities of 10,000 men for each of six hours per day. This job again involved many contacts with officers and was "well adapted to the Chatwell personality." He progressed in steps to the rank of sergeant, but throughout he used all possible means to secure officer training.

Eventually Chatwell was sent to Officers Candidate School, where he lived, as a cadet, a regimented "but withal a stimulating and healthful life." Here he ex-

pressed no motivational problem for "the competition is keen and real, as opposed to the ivory tower which so irked me in college." He was eager not only to succeed but to excel and summed up this experience as follows: "Real discipline backed up by excellent motivation produced a systematic, determined, conscientious Chatwell."

Chatwell commented on the procedures used by the Army for personnel utilization. The system, which "nauseated" him, was in the hands of "ignorant people who are arbitrary or dishonest." The system was all right for "a guy like me who asks for what he wants."

Immediately upon receipt of his commission, Chatwell became an instructor at the same school at which he trained. He became bored with this position which lacked "academic freedom and incentive." Having improved his material position, however, he now became engaged. His family gave their blessings and his father sent him "a rock as big as a good-sized pea."

At this time Chatwell signed up as a glider pilot and was awaiting orders. He might be sent away before his wedding, and although he was deeply in love, he was restless for some action. He never became a glider pilot and stayed on instead as an instructor for eight months. He was promoted to first lieutenant, was married, and was sent to intelligence school for a six-week course. There followed duty as an intelligence officer in several units in the United States. Chatwell's first child, a son, was born during this period. Chatwell was elevated to the rank of captain.

Later Chatwell was sent overseas where he had long periods of idleness for contemplation, alternating with periods of great activity. "A very natural re-evaluation" of what was important ensued. Listing the important things, Chatwell included food, independence, warmth, dryness, affection of women, the opportunity for productive work, liquor, and tobacco. His daydreaming involved two fantasies. One wish was to become as quickly as possible economically independent, as distinguished from financially independent, by a combination of farming and manufacture on a unitary, self-sufficient basis. He studied texts on agriculture and planned the whole project "field by field down to the last shovel of manure." He shared a tent with a doctor and together they "worked" on the farm and its management. His other dream concerned entering politics.

The actual activities Chatwell engaged in at this time included digging wells, building bridges and roads, organizing water supplies, supervising radio and telephone communications, and trying court-martial cases. He remarked, "I must say one of the most satisfying things I know of is to go into a jungle and set up a reasonable degree of civilization there with your own hands—water, light, sanitation, and so forth." This experience convinced him he could make a go of the self-sufficient farming and manufacturing establishment. This plan he shared with his wife, via mail.

Upon his return to civilian life, Chatwell first investigated farming, but dismissed this plan as foolishness, "since it appeared that farm prices would prob-

ably fall faster in the next few years than even the best farmer could create wealth." His next plan was to get a job in a chemical plant and learn how to run such a business "so that when the time came I could move to a farm, set up the chemical business, and start in on both simultaneously." He was unable to find what he wanted and finally he "began to regress to my first love . . . patent law."

Two jobs became available to him at this time, both offering adequate starting salaries. One job was with a large chemical company in their patent department and Chatwell rejected this in favor of the practice of patent law in a small, private law firm. He acknowledged that the corporation position would be more secure and might lead to the farm plan, but he was at this time more concerned with independence. As an alternate to patent law, he might go into general law practice within this firm and eventually fulfill his "ultimate ambition in politics."

Chatwell started on this job and enrolled in law school, evenings. His program called for eight semesters, five nights a week. School, Chatwell reported, was wonderful and for the first time in his life, he looked forward to classes and believed he was at or near the head of his class. He said of law school, "I am in my element when it comes to tearing a case apart and finding out what makes it tick. And, as you know, I am not unaffected by the sound of my own voice and therefore, I get a big kick out of the class discussions." The method of teaching consisted of the teacher calling upon a student to give an oral presentation of a case and then needling and criticizing him as a judge needles counsel in court. Chatwell said you never knew when you might be called upon so that you prepared every case very carefully. When he knew he had to stand on his feet before a class and defend himself, he needed no further motivation to work hard. As an undergraduate, Chatwell remembered, he never felt it was important to do well in studies, because these were divorced from reality. Chatwell felt the lecture system at Harvard was to be blamed and recommended it be abandoned. Chatwell told of an instance of losing his temper at law school. He spoke more than any of the other students and was called upon to answer questions no one else could answer. One time, when Chatwell asked a question, the instructor answered so as to make Chatwell feel the instructor had underestimated him and "his blood boiled." Chatwell started talking and "kept right on talking, almost like in a dream." The instructor was very angry.

Chatwell was very enthusiastic about his work which offered great variety involving the fringe of scientific development "to stimulate the imagination," the ancient wisdom of the law, and "constant strife and argument to exact care and method from my disorderly soul." He worked with great intensity and interest at the varied tasks and each task could be completed and filed until it was needed later.

The gang at the office Chatwell found "first-rate." "They accept me, in all my ignorance, as one of them; they are patient with me and are kind to my ego, both when I fail and when I succeed. And I succeed." The youngest of the group at the law firm was

at least fifteen years older than Chatwell and so he saw a bright future for himself. All of these men knew much more than he and he became more willing to listen to others and to accept his own limitations. On the other hand, he has continued to feel confident that he "knows more about some things" than they do.

Chatwell was happy in his work, but could not have been interested if it did not appeal to his "combativeness." Chatwell described himself as lethargic when not stimulated. "I can loaf around and daydream for hours with no trouble. But my work excites me." He recognized that he required "a certain amount of opposition to keep me going. Otherwise I'm apt to flag off." Fortunately, then, "the law is a jealous mistress," he said.

Chatwell noted that he tended to identify himself with the client quite enthusiastically, particularly where the development was interesting to him. This was especially true if the clients were "small fellows who are just starting out." He found in such cases, he was talking about "we this" and "we that."

Chatwell spoke of his need to be "independent of the system." "Law," he said, "represents the procedural aspects of obtaining liberty." And again, the study of law "tends to make for a more conscious drawing-up of the limitations that the organization of society imposes on us."

The ideas of economic independence and self-sufficiency still appeal to Chatwell. He was not insecure in his present position. "Barring some remarkable catastrophe" his job was nearly recession-proof and during the last economic upset "they didn't feel a thing in there (the law firm). It's safe."

There was a little dissatisfaction, however, with his profession in Chatwell's mind. "In law, like most professions when you get down to it, we're parasites to a certain extent. Someday I might do a little manufacturing or farming or just something that's productive, you see . . . that's purely productive. . . . But there is still the fact that you can't eat what the lawyer makes—right away. You have to change it into something else first."

Chatwell now set up a subgoal: "To get through law school, be admitted to the bar, and achieve a measure of competency in the profession. That's the immediate goal."

Beyond that he saw several alternatives. "When I'm through school and prices have come back to normal, we buy a farm. If it later appears attractive to add a manufactory, that can be done. On the other hand, the door of politics remains open, too." His reason for going into politics was given thus: "I've often felt that if you criticize the way George is doing it, you should stand prepared to do it yourself if the occasion arises." Chatwell said he didn't insist "on being President of the U. S. or anything of that sort." He might, however, some day run for the state legislature. Such plans were still tentative. A third prospect for the future involved education. "One of the other obligations that I think a man should have is, that if he criticizes educators, he should also be prepared to take over some education. I would like to teach constitutional law—perhaps one or three hours per week. Not to make any money out of it because

I don't know anybody who ever made money that way, but because I feel that it's a thing that should be done and I know there's a need for it."

Interpretation: Chatwell's career and personality. From the foregoing, exclusively the conscious descriptions of Chatwell's views of his world and life and ideals given over a period of eight years, a personality emerges and the career can be seen in the context of the salient life thema and typical adjustive strategies. What are the important variables for this personality?

For Chatwell, independence had long been a highly valued ideal, emphasized by his mother in her child-rearing practices, exemplified by his father in his own educational and professional pursuits, and asserted by Chatwell as a major determinant in his choice of both profession and position. The almost ideal background of family solidarity can in itself generate the need for autonomy. This need for independence or autonomy appeared to arise as well from a press which was at times arbitrary, aggressive, or dominating. Chatwell's father was described as dogmatic and highly nervous and Chatwell encountered other "systems" too, which were perceived as capricious, unjust, and so forth. One way of reacting to such systems was to become free of them and Chatwell's recurrent idea of the independent farm-manufactory would be a career-type of adjustment to fulfill such a need for autonomy.

The need for autonomy was, however, in conflict with another need, to be dependent and protected.

Chatwell spoke of his ideal of "home and rest" and he once wrote in his freshman theme on growth about the longing to lay down one's load at the feet of a stronger and wiser person. Independence required effort, risk, and responsibility and from Chatwell's Thematic Apperception Test productions one could infer a preconscious need (Leary's Level III) for succorance. The heroes of these stories were in many instances reduced by circumstances such as illness or accident to accept help and sympathy, to be excused from effort, or to be praised for lesser accomplishments. This need was, in general, not acceptable to Chatwell at a conscious level and he rated himself quite low on "dependence" in a self-rating scale. His highest rating on 23 needs he gave to "autonomy."

How did this conflict get resolved, if indeed it did, in Chatwell's career? He chose a profession which represented to him "the procedural aspects of obtaining liberty," and he decided that of two jobs, the one which granted more immediate independence was his choice. However, for support, there was "the ancient wisdom of the law" and the gang of older men at the office who accepted him. (Erikson suggests that the struggle for autonomy can be a jealous rage directed most often against encroachments by younger siblings. In Chatwell's office there were no younger men.) Chatwell seemed to be aware of his own growth in this environment, as he could begin to accept his own limitations and listen to others who knew "more than I will know for many years." With maturation in this favorable setting, Chatwell needed no longer be so assertive about independence and could accept his limitations of abilities in general. His self-ratings on abilities in the second study were in quite a few instances adjusted downwards in an apparently more realistic self-assessment, so that he could now admit, as he had not been willing to as an undergraduate, to some abilities which were "below average" (that is, physical and art-creative abilities).

Chatwell's law firm provided safety and protection from the larger arbitrary economic system in that it had been untouched by previous recessions. "Barring a catastrophe," the needs for independence and dependence could be met simultaneously.

Argument was, for Chatwell, a highly enjoyed activity in which he excelled. He had in his early life been able to align himself with his mother and oppose his rivals, his father and his brother, in a socially acceptable way. Talking and arguing allowed for the intrusion into other people's ears and minds and could be an expression of the needs for aggression and dominance. Chatwell had the necessary verbal fluency and conjunctivity and with his very superior intelligence (his Wechsler Bellevue IQ was 142) and retentive memory he collected facts to use almost as weapons. (Chatwell's performance on the Graduate Record Examination exceeded the average in all subject-matter fields, his scores averaging 130 points above the means.) A developed competence in argument was enjoyed in itself but also allowed for a certain amount of display. A rather crude need for exhibitionism, which was expressed on the preconscious level in Chatwell's TAT stories, and again inferred from his enthusiasm as a subject in the clinic demonstrations, was thus given expression in argument. And according to Chatwell's perceptions, argument was a masculine activity for he found it "only natural" for men engaged in studying the abstract to argue. There was evidence of a compensatory element in this kind of cleverness, for example, in a thematic completion test story, where the hero, unable to attain the kind of success his father had achieved in football, instead objected to the way the sport was organized and threw himself wholeheartedly into modifying the sport and found he had "just the qualifications for successfully doing this." Chatwell, then, used argument to express aggression to gain dominance, to exhibit his talents, and to be masculine in the way he could be. Situations in which he could practice this skill were "duck soup" for him. At college argument served him in only a very limited way and he observed "the teacher must win." He was a mediocre and disinterested student in the ivory tower. Another thematic completion test story tells of a hero living away from home while at college and "instead of the good-natured attack which he had been led to expect when he brought home a new idea or skill, he was met with strong silence, openmouthed amazement, or shocked disapproval." And Chatwell failed in one very important instance "to bring his powers to bear" on the public-speaking instructor at Harvard. Thereafter, and for the duration of his career in the Army, he seemed to lose interest in argument and also in his long-term professional goal, law. With marriage and the masculine role of the Army officer, with real and keen competi-

tion in the training, with teaching and other outlets for display, argument seemed to decline as an important activity. Also, other needs became pre-eminent in his situation overseas and the goals of food, body comforts, and independence could be better filled by the farm-manufactory plan. When this plan was abandoned or postponed because of the economic situation and also perhaps because of the autonomy-dependence conflict (did he really want to be *that* independent?), Chatwell enrolled in law school and came to understand what strong motivation was involved in argument. He had a necessary outlet for his "combativeness." And further, he seemed to feel that without such strife, he would succumb to laziness. (In the fantasy productions there was evidence of a considerable attraction to passivity and rest.) In the process of being "needled by a judge or teacher," Chatwell could respond at his best. He did extremely well in the stress interview of the second study in which he defended his opinions which were attacked. His best productions in the Rorschach Test were in small details and in the use of white spaces. The latter use is interpreted by Klopfer (Klopfer, *et al.*, 1954) as an expression of oppositional tendencies and in this kind of expression Chatwell could do his best. These abilities combined with a mind that was assessed as able to perform good abstract as well as perceptual thinking made Chatwell especially well-suited for his choice of law.

There were many manifestations of Chatwell's interest in things mechanical and scientific. He remembered playing with tools as a little child, he was interested in radio broadcasting and sound reproduction as hobbies, and he found a large number of man-made objects in the Rorschach Test. With an aptitude for science he could not, like his hero in the football story, be a scientist but he could nevertheless enjoy the stimulation of being on the fringe of scientific developments. He could not compete so directly with his father but felt also that science was too ivory tower, isolated from people and argument. With the practice of patent law he could vindicate the injustices suffered by his father from the system. He could identify himself with the "small fellow" and thus, feeling like an inventor, could fight against the injustice of the system.

Chatwell made some happy adjustments in his chosen career. There was some dissatisfaction with it, however, as he perceived the absence of productivity. He valued this attribute in his father and considered himself a "parasite." This dissatisfaction might indeed some day motivate Chatwell to buy a farm or factory or both. More likely hobbies and collaboration on some scientific inventions would fulfill this need for productivity. For the time, this remained a need unfulfilled by his career.

Politics remained an ultimate goal for Chatwell at the end of this study. That he would expose himself to a political campaign seems unlikely. He avoided college politics and the debating team and there seemed to be an unaccepted latent avoidance need. Chatwell would avoid the shame, humiliation, or ridicule that most likely would be encountered in a bitter political campaign. We remember that his "blood boiled" when he thought an instructor underestimated him. On the other hand, in a very civilized political structure, in an appointive post, or in a district where there was minimal opposition Chatwell might run and enter politics.

The education goal appears more likely, for this was an area in which Chatwell had already achieved success and would look for further success here. Teaching law would allow for the expression of many of his needs although it too was not "productive" and was not well-remunerated.

Chatwell's career appeared to offer at least a temporary solution for his independence-dependence conflict and allowed for the argument which was so important in Chatwell's performance and well-being. It was a field which brought him close to science without his actual participation in scientific endeavor. To the extent that he could maintain the respect and praise of those around him, he would most likely persevere in this choice which was suited to one of his "mental ability and temperament." Dissatisfaction arising from the lack of productivity might be overcome with an avocation.

Conclusions

The procedures used by the Harvard Psychological Clinic to study first, the problems of normal adolescence and later, the relationship of opinions and personality have been useful, as well, for the study of the career. Autobiographies and interviews in which the subjects have been encouraged to talk about those things which are of greatest importance to them yield much information about career decisions and other goal-striving activities, and the regularities of functioning become evident. The important variables for the individual personality and his career emerge. As for vocational development in the individual case, personality traits and thema bear an important relationship to vocational preference, entry, success, and satisfaction. The one subject reported here has, in the context of his career, coped with a central conflict of his personality and found an outlet for a highly cathected activity. An unmet need gives rise to dissatisfaction with the career and the question of perseveration of choice is raised.

Bibliography

Bidwell, C. E., and McArthur, C. C. *"Values, Careers and Higher Education: A Comparison of Two Generations of Harvard Undergraduates,"* mimeo (Cambridge: the authors, Harvard University, 1960).

Hall, C. S., and Lindzey, G. *Theories of Personality* (New York: John Wiley and Sons, Inc., 1957).

Klopfer, Bruno, Ainsworth, Mary D., Klopfer, Walter G., and Holt, Robert R. *Developments in the Rorschach Technique,* Vol. 1 (New York: World Book Company, 1954).

Leary, Timothy. *Interpersonal Diagnosis of Personality* (New York: The Ronald Press, 1957).

Murray, H. A. *Explorations in Personality* (New York: Oxford University Press, 1938).

Smith, M. B., Bruner, J. S., and White, R. W. *Opinions and Personality* (New York: John Wiley and Sons, Inc., 1956).